do good

HOW DESIGN CAN CHANGE THE WORLD

David B. Berman, FGDC, R.G.D.

San Francisco, California | February 2013

Why does this book need a title page? Why repeat what is already on the cover? The publisher says we have to have a title page for historical reasons and copyright issues. Maybe someone should tell publishers: if we removed the title page from every book published, we could save, on average, 3.1 billion pages of paper a year in the United States alone.

Speaking of saving paper, if you wish to share this book without giving yours away, bear in mind that **it can be purchased at safari.peachpit.com in ebook format.** But wait: According to BBC Two, data farms now use as much energy as the entire car manufacturing industry. And the store of knowledge is doubling every five years. By 2020, the carbon emissions produced in generating energy for the Internet will be the equivalent of those produced by the airline industry. Tough choices: read the book.

Do Good ~~Design~~

How Design Can Change the World

Author: David B. Berman, FGDC, R.G.D.
Publisher: Nancy Aldrich-Ruenzel
Project Editor: Michael Nolan
Development Editor: Margaret S. Anderson
Contributing Editors: Reva Berman and Sabina Lysnes
Graphic Design and Typography: Cynthia Hoffos FGDC, with David B. Berman and Erik Spiekermann
Production Editor: David Van Ness
Layout/Compositing: Cynthia Hoffos and Khadija Safri
Cover Photography/Illustration: Trevor Johnston
Researchers: Patrick Cunningham and Dr. S. Berman
Copy Editor: Haig MacGregor
Indexer: Heather McNeill
Product Marketing Manager: Sara Jane Todd
Publicity Manager: Laura Pexton
Design Manager: Charlene Will
Manufacturing Coordinator: Jason Perrone
~~Proofreader~~ proofreditor!: Rose Weisburd
Fonts: Erik Spiekermann (Meta Serif, Meta Plus) and Albert Jan-Pool (DIN Pro)[1]

New Riders
1249 Eighth Street
Berkeley, CA 94710 U.S.A
510/524-2178
510/524-2221 (fax)

Published in association with AIGA Design Press.

Find us on the Web at:
www.newriders.com

To report errors, please send a note to errata@peachpit.com

New Riders is an imprint of Peachpit, a division of Pearson Education.

Copyright © 2009, 2013 by David Berman

ISBN 13: 978-0-321-57320-9
ISBN 10: 0-321-57320-X

9 8 7 6 5 4 3 2 1

Printed and bound in the United States of America.

Notice of Rights: All rights reserved. No part of this book may be reproduced or transmitted in any form by any means, electronic, mechanical, photocopying, recording, or otherwise, without the prior written permission of the publisher. For information on getting permission for reprints and excerpts, contact permissions@peachpit.com.

Notice of Liability: The information in this book is distributed on an "As Is" basis without warranty. While every precaution has been taken in the preparation of the book, neither the author nor Peachpit shall have any liability to any person or entity with respect to any loss or damage caused or alleged to be caused directly or indirectly by the instructions contained in this book.

Trademarks: Many of the designations used by manufacturers and sellers to distinguish their products are claimed as trademarks. Where those designations appear in this book, and Peachpit was aware of a trademark claim, the designations appear as requested by the owner of the trademark. All other product names and services identified throughout this book are used in editorial fashion only and for the benefit of such companies with no intention of infringement of the trademark. No such use, or the use of any trade name, is intended to convey endorsement or other affiliation with this book.

Sharpie® Permanent Marker appears courtesy of Sanford Corporation.

CONTENTS

Non fate solo buon design,
ma fate del bene.

Nedělej jen dobrý design, dělej ho pro dobro věci.

لا تصمم جيداً فقط،
بل افعل جيداً

Não faça solo buon design. Faça o bem.

좋은 디자인만 하지 말고
좋은 일을 하라!

Don't just do good design... do good!

デザインだけではなく、本当に「良い」ものを

Ne csak jó design-t csinálj, hanem tégy jót is vele!

Gør ikke bare
godt design,
gør det
godt!

Ne faites pas
que du bon design,
faites du
bien!

Gjør ikke bare god design,
gjør noe godt!

אל תעשה עיצוב טוב בלבד,
עשה גם טוב!

Nicht nur tun,
gutes
Design,
die Gutes
tun.

Delatje dobro,
ne samo
dobrega oblikovanja.

¡No hagas sólo buen diseño,
haz el bien!

做好设计不够，还须行善有益。

I've written "Don't just do good design… do good!" in the prevailing language of each place this journey has taken me to. (So if yours is missing, invite me over!)

Do Good Design is now available in Simplified Chinese, Korean, and Indonesian, as well as English. If you would like this book published in additional languages, contact us.

To D.o.M. and D.o.D.
for instilling in me the knowledge
that social justice is not optional.

... and thank you to Naomi Klein
for urging me to write this book.

सिर्फ अच्छा डिज़ाइन नहीं,
अच्छा करें।

Gwnewch fwy na dylunio da — gwnewch ddaioni

Ná ach ttach bhfuil dea-dheargan, a dhéanamh go maith!

Älä tee vain hyvää designia ... tee hyvää!

صرف اچھی ڈیزائن نہ کرو ... اچھا کرو

Jangan hanya buat desain yang keren,
tapi buatlah desain yang mendorong kebaikan

Sukurti gera dizaina per maža. Kurk gėrį!

不僅要做好的設計，更需心存善念。

How we chose to manufacture this book

This book was printed and bound by Courier Corporation, in Terre Haute, Indiana. We chose Courier for their commitment to responsible, sustainable manufacturing.

Courier is certified to the Forest Stewardship Council™ (FSC®). The goals of the FSC involve detailing objectives for the protection of endangered species, wildlife, soil quality, and water quality. The FSC is an international network, founded in 1993 by environmental groups concerned with global tropical deforestation and unsustainable logging practices.

Courier is also certified by the Sustainable Forestry Initiative (SFI), and the Programme for the Endorsement of Forestry Certification (PEFC).

The paper in this book is certified by Rainforest Alliance to the FSC chain of custody standard. We used vegetable-based inks and optimized the page imposition to minimize waste (using suctioning for all trim, and recycling of all waste paper and plates). Bleeds (ink that runs off the edges of pages) did not cause additional paper use, due to the shaving required by the finishing process.

Why we chose Mohawk paper

We chose the papers for this book based on their high post-consumer waste content and FSC certifications. The text pages are Mohawk Options 100% PC White Vellum 80 Text, containing 100% postconsumer waste fiber. The cover stock is Mohawk Everyday Digital Coated Gloss White 100C.

All papers were manufactured by Mohawk Paper in Cohoes, New York. Mohawk is North America's largest privately owned manufacturer of fine papers, envelopes, and specialty substrates for commercial and digital printing. This family-owned business has consistently renewed its commitment to environmental stewardship. Mohawk was the first U.S. manufacturer of commercial printing papers to match 100% of its electricity with windpower renewable energy credits and the first U.S. premium paper mill to shift toward carbon-neutral production.

Why we chose New Riders and AIGA to publish this book

New Riders is part of Pearson, a global company that is committed to social responsibility and making a positive impact on the world. Pearson includes many brands you've likely heard of: Peachpit Press, the Financial Times Group, the Penguin Group, and DK Travel Guides. Pearson also partners with Safari Books Online (safari.peachpit.com), which is helping to save forests by publishing electronically. Both Pearson and David Berman achieved climate-neutrality in 2009. Pearson supports the Anne Frank Trust, and is a signatory to the UN Global Compact. Particularly admirable is their Made With Care initiative, which calls for publishers to produce their product using the most ethical and environmentally-friendly processes possible. Visit http://pearson.com/environment for Pearson's full environmental policy.

AIGA Design Press is a partnership of New Riders and AIGA, the professional association for design. AIGA's mission is to advance designing as a professional craft, strategic tool, and vital cultural force. AIGA is also committed to imparting the value of sustainable design at every level of practice and production.

FOREWORD

by Erik Spiekermann

PHOTO: SUSANNA DULKINYS

When the *First Things First* manifesto from 1964 was about to be republished by *Adbusters* for the new millennium, I readily signed it. As the manifesto put it, "designers... apply their skill and imagination to sell dog biscuits, designer coffee, diamonds, detergents, hair gel, cigarettes, credit cards, sneakers, butt toners, light beer and heavy-duty recreational vehicles." Who wouldn't agree with the conclusion that "our skills could be put to worthwhile use"? I signed, because the list of colleagues and friends who had already signed was impressive, even intimidating. And the original signatories from 1964 were pretty much all my heroes.

I did, however, add a paragraph stating slight misgivings. It is easy, after all, to put your name on a list of famous designers and bask in the reflected glow of their presence. But does that change what we would do in our studio the next morning? Would I tell my 70-some employees that from now on, we would be do-gooders only, send our "commercial" clients away and wait for more worthy projects to find the way to our door? Didn't the other signatories also do work for hire, for clients who use our work to sell more of whatever they are selling? Is all selling bad? Is designing books always good because there are no bad books? Designing signage for a public transit system is good, airport signage is bad because only The Rich can afford to fly? And how about signage for shopping centers? Bad? Amusement parks?

As opposed to architects, who honestly think that the world would cease to exist if they stopped working, we graphic designers know that the world would probably carry on pretty much the same without our services. Things may look a little less colorful and some companies might sell less without our help in communicating their services or goods, but lives will not be lost. There are, however, situations where graphic design, or rather the lack of it, has cost lives. In 1997, a fire raged through Düsseldorf airport in Germany. Thick smoke made it difficult to see the emergency signs, which were also not placed where they should have been, too small, and too badly lit. Sixteen people died because they could not find their way out. As a result, we were hired to not only design new signage that was legible, well-lit, and visually appealing, but we also worked with the planners to make sure the signs were put where they would be visible. The architects wanted the signs "out of the way of the beautiful architecture," as they put it, which would have repeated the previous mistakes. We had to insist that we were not hired to simply make the place pretty, but actually make the airport function properly. Behaving responsibly is not asked for in Requests for Proposals, but without asking questions that haven't even been asked, we would just be window dressers.

My first responsibility is to my family and to my extended family, the employees of my studio. They look to me for their livelihood. They all became designers because they wanted to make something – something that was better than what had been there before. Of course we discuss what sort of projects we take on and what type of clients we work for. Some issues are quickly resolved: we wouldn't work for a cigarette brand, although some of us still smoke. But we have worked for automotive brands, and most of us still have cars, although essentially cars are very, very bad.

Whether what we design is good or bad is difficult to judge. We live in this society, and we benefit from the material wealth it offers. As Max Bill put it, we apply 90 percent of our efforts to making something work, and we should apply the remaining 10 percent to making it beautiful. "Designers have enormous power to influence how we see our world, and how we live our lives," David writes in this book. I could not agree more, and I think that we all need to be constantly aware of what we do, for whom we work, and how our work affects others. But whatever our good intentions may be, we cannot ignore the reality that design is a business and has to live by the rules of business. As we have seen recently, **those rules need to be rewritten.** There is hope for more awareness and responsibility, even in the world of commerce that we'd rather not belong to but cannot escape from.

In my 30 years of running a design studio, I have come to the conclusion that there is one thing we can do that nobody can stop us from. We alone decide *how* we work. Whatever the restrictions and limitations of the commercial world that buys our services, we create our own processes. *How* we deal with our employees, our suppliers, our clients, our peers, and even our competitors is totally up to us. How we make something is very important, and it is the one thing we can influence without much interference. We'd still have to fill out tax returns, make sure the computers are running and the rent is paid, but the way we work with each other and with our clients is where we can be different. As we take in the big picture of what this book is all about, let's begin by looking at our immediate reality. Charity starts at home.

Erik Spiekermann is an author, information designer, and typographer. He founded MetaDesign and FontShop, is Honorary Professor at the University of the Arts in Bremen, and has an honorary doctorship from Pasadena Art Center. He was the first designer to be elected into the Hall of Fame by the European Design Awards for Communication Design. He lives and works in Berlin, London, and San Francisco. His studio, Spiekermann Partners, employs 30 designers.

FOREWORD TO THE CHINESE EDITION[2]

by Min Wang

PHOTO: ZHENG BIN

In 2006, David Berman gave a lecture at our School of Design in Beijing. It resonated for both teachers and students because it reflected keenly on the work, the responsibilities, and the identity of the designer, touching on the school's slogan: "Design for the People." Afterward, I told him my hope that this book would be published in China someday. A huge design industry was born of our booming economy, almost overnight. Thousands of designers tirelessly service the economic engine, sparing no time to think of David's issues. This book will cause our designers to explore who they are and what they do.

Perhaps we chose to be designers to create beautiful objects. But do we bring something unexpectedly negative to society, along with that beauty? Are we helping make our environment unlivable?

We think of ourselves as designers, not decision makers; lacking a strong voice to change society's behaviors. We fail to admit our responsibility for the decline of the natural environment. We must reevaluate, and discover our share of influence.

We are often urged to put commercial interests first. But when one re-examines our social responsibility, you see the truth in David Berman's words: to do good rather than just do good design benefits both society and the enterprise.

It's an honor to be a colleague of David's on the Icograda board. David pushes designers around the world to reflect on their duties, and to design for universal access. His actions have a large influence on many people, and thus on the global environment.

Design that is conducive to the planet and to humanity is good design. Design that is aesthetic and benevolent is good design. In the end, we must bring these aspects together.

Min Wang is dean of the Central Academy of Fine Arts School of Design, China's premier design school, and design director for the 2008 Beijing Olympics.

LETTER FROM AIGA
by Richard Grefé

PHOTO: AIGA

AIGA is publishing this vital reflection on the power of design because David Berman understands – and communicates with such intensity, sincerity, and clarity – that creativity has the potential not only to defeat habit, but also to affect positive change.

AIGA's connection with David's indomitable esprit and steadfast commitment to social principles occurred when he brought to my attention the environmental and social standards he had advocated for Canadian designers. Milton Glaser, who has long had a similar commitment to the responsibilities of designers, joined me in adapting AIGA's standards of professional practices to David's language, adding the responsibilities that a designer has to his or her audience. Now, David's perspective is at the core of the designer's ethos in North America.

> "This instrument can teach, it can illuminate; yes, and it can even inspire, but it can do so only to the extent that humans are determined to use it to those ends. Otherwise it is merely wires and lights in a box."
>
> EDWARD R. MURROW (1908–1965)
> March 15, 1954, speaking about television

In 2008, AIGA China published the standards in Chinese, where there are one million students just beginning their design careers, and these standards are the only expression of professional expectations.

Margaret Mead had it right: "Never doubt that a small group of thoughtful, committed citizens can change the world. Indeed, it is the only thing that ever has." Let's see what David's very public statement, this book, can do to change our expectations.

Creativity can defeat habit. And we are counting on it.

Richard Grefé is executive director of AIGA,
the professional association for design in the United States.

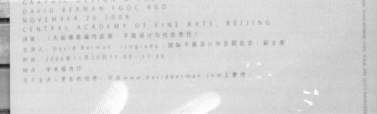

GRAPHIC DESIGN & SOCIAL RESPONSIBILITY
DAVID BERMAN FGDC RGD
NOVEMBER 20 2006
CENTRAL ACADEMY OF FINE ARTS, BEIJING
讲座：《大规模欺骗性武器：平面设计与社会责任》
主讲人：David Berman，Icograda（国际平面设计协会联合会）副主席
时间：2006年11月20日15:00-17:30
地点：学术报告厅
关于主讲人更多的信息，可在www.davidberman.com上参考

WEAPONS OF MASS DECEPTION

❝❝ Over **NINETY-FIVEPERCENT** ofthedesignerswhohaveeverlivedarealivetoday.Together, we have the power to define what professionalism in the communications design field will be about: helping increase market share or helping repair the world. There are more than **ONE AND A HALF MILLION** graphic designers in the World today. Imagine what we could achieve if each one of us spent just **TEN PERCENT** of our professional time on projects that will help build a better future: together, that's over **SIX MILLION** hours a week! There is so much power in visuals and when we use that power to deceive people,

Promotional poster for speech in Beijing, December 2006 [3]

…s is the largest bandwidth pipe into the human brain and we visual communicators are the people who design what goes in. We have a responsibility to not mess with that

PHOTO: DAVID BERMAN

A designer is

INTRODUCTION

IN THE YEAR 2000, I sold the successful graphic design agency I had founded at the age of 22. I chose a new career path, to achieve a balance between working for clients who are helping repair the world and sharing how to do that with others.

This book is a reflection of that quest. Its message is not just for designers and those who consume design, but for all professionals.

Graphic designers (some say "communication designers")[4] create a bridge between information and understanding. Industrial designers add usability and appeal to objects. Interior designers and architects invent where we live.

Designers have an essential social responsibility because design is at the core of the world's largest challenges... and solutions. Designers create so much of the world we live in, the things we consume, and the expectations we seek to fulfill. They shape what we see, what we use, and what we waste. Design has enormous power to influence how we engage our world, and how we envision our future. How much power? I intend to shock you.

Everyone is now a designer. We live in an era that encourages us to develop our very own personalized interfaces with the world. Each time you resize your Web browser window, DVR your television programming, build a playlist, or customize a ringtone, you join a design team. Add in the crowdsourcing technologies of Web 2.0, and your role becomes far broader. Indeed, **I believe that the future of our world is now our common design project.**

Those who know me are aware that until now I've been a designer, a strategist, an expert speaker on a mission... but not a book author.

"an emerging synthesis of artist, inventor, mechanic,

Within the low-tech medium of a book, I'm told that, no matter how intrigued you may be with these words and pictures, there is over a 70 percent chance that you won't finish reading it. And I can't corner you in the hallway later, as I could if you slipped out on one of my presentations. Because you may wander from this book and unintentionally never return, I want to share the essence of my argument right now.

So before you get distracted by your iPad, a tweet, or someone texts or even calls you for dinner, here are the core thoughts:

Designers have far more power than they realize: their creativity fuels the most efficient (and most destructive) tools of deception in human history.

The largest threat to humanity's future just may be the consumption of more than necessary. We are caught up in an unsustainable frenzy, spurred by rapid advances in the sophistication, psychology, speed, and reach of visual lies designed to convince us we "need" more stuff than we really do.

Human civilization, trending toward one global civilization, cannot afford to make even one more major global mistake.

The same design that fuels mass overconsumption also holds the power to repair the world.

We live in an unprecedented technological age, where we can each leave a larger legacy by propagating our best ideas than by propagating our chromosomes.

Designers can be a model for other professionals for identifying one's sphere of influence, and then embrace the responsibility that accompanies that power to help repair the world.

So don't just do good design, do good.

objective economist and evolutionary strategist."
BUCKMINSTER FULLER (1895–1983)

I am going to share with you how we can use design to help repair (or destroy) our civilization. The specifics are pertinent to all design and communications fields, while the principles of how one can make a difference are transferable to any profession. With my graphic design background, I draw most of my examples from what I know best: graphic design, advertising, and branding.

There has never been a better nor more important time to discuss responsible design. Back in 2002, I had my first chance to speak outside my native Canada, at an international design conference in the Czech Republic. My *How Logo Can We Go?* speech was a maverick[5] presentation, the only one about socially responsible design. Just five years later, I moderated the social responsibility themed day at the Icograda World Design Congress in Cuba, and almost every speaker *every* day tied their work to the difference that designers can make for the world. In 20 countries, I've seen, heard, and felt the change that is in motion globally. But will the shift be too little, too late?

Designers who publish books usually show you their designs. But in this volume, I'll instead focus on the work of others: some of the most influential design of our age. While you probably won't know the designers' names, you will recognize their work.

At the end, I will make an appeal to your true self. Don't panic: I won't ask you to give up your job, earn less money, or even have less fun. I *will* ask you to commit to becoming part of the solution.

If you're already convinced but short on time, then skip now to the pledge on page 146.

Otherwise, as with most design problems, the place to start is in defining the goals, challenges, and constraints: doing so is typically more than half the solution. So here follows the "creative brief" for the design challenge of our lifetimes.

the creative

disarming the weapons

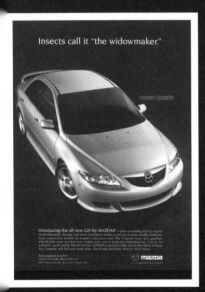

Insects call it "the widowmaker."

Introducing the all-new 220-hp MAZDA6

mazda

秋葉原発!
萌えの
マンゴーケーキバー
moe no
mango cake bar

rvine, California:
When did roadkill become something to celebrate? We make 73 species extinct every day. Can we not show more respect for those hat survive despite us? This ad copy promises to boost your confidence, as you master weaker things. How did cars go from

Tokyo, Japan:
I found this food packaging for mango-flavored snack cakes in a grocery store in Japan. The food is as simple as it comes. However, the package design is layered with complexity, bordering on the predatory. Is most shopping simply feeding a frustrated

brief:
of mass deception

Montréal, Canada:
Tobacco marketers greedily circumvent laws banning point-of purchase cigarette displays in stores, encouraging corner store owners to instead display clever matchboxes that mimic cigarette packs on the checkout counter. Must the marketing ethic be as unhealthy as the product?

Suva, Fiji:
Convincing people to pay more for water than for refined gasoline may seem impressive. Shipping water from the South Seas in plastic bottles from China to the U.S. and Europe in container ships seems unsustainable. Positioning the product as an environmental solution seems outrageous.

enjoy Shaker with a twist...

Cult Shaker transit ad, Copenhagen. Cheap caffeine, alcohol, and sex in a bottle

PHOTO: DAVID BERMAN

> # "If we do not change our direction, we are likely to end up where we are headed." CHINESE PROVERB

1 START NOW

IMAGINE FOR A MOMENT that you're just over 20 years old. You know exactly what you want to do with your life: you've found your passion. You're proudly paying your own bills doing what you love. Life is good.

I first discovered my passion publishing a magazine in high school. At University of Waterloo, it was all-nighters at the student paper, neglecting my degree program in computer science. By the late 1980s, I had followed my muse to a tiny design studio above a pawnshop in old Ottawa South. Like so many other young people who realize that designing is who they are, I was jazzed with creating, exploring, and pushing the limits of my perfect little world-within-a-world of grids, fonts, and Pantone® colors, long before desktop publishing would make such terms household words.

PHOTO: STEVE EICHLER

In front of David Berman Typographics, Hopewell Avenue, 1988

I could shut out the messy world, and strive to surround myself with beautifully designed things. There was delight in staying up all night spinning two-inch font filmstrips through my Typositor, hand-rolling adhesive wax onto phototype galleys, refining kerning pairs, and unavoidably breathing photo chemicals. X-Acto blades, Letraset, and Rubylith... in the morning, I would zoom around town with a huge portfolio case strapped to my bright-red scooter, wearing cotton crayon shoes and all-black everything else.

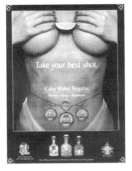

So when that hot[6] feminist girlfriend tore into my microcosm, claiming that graphic designers like me were responsible for destroying forests in support of the systematic objectification of women by using pictures of their bodies to help sell products... well, my first reaction was to deny everything. But then I took notice of example after example, and promised to do something about it.

A youthful, creative, male mix of social justice, lust, and angry young hubris naively scooted me off to my first-ever meeting of the local chapter of the Society of Graphic Designers of Canada. Hastily written eco-feminist manifesto clutched in my hand, I was intent on changing the code of ethics of my profession. Little did I know that ride would span 16 years and take me to more than 30 countries and counting, vastly surpassing my naïve expectations. But more on that later ...

March, 1988
Presented in writing and verbally to the GDC Ottawa Chapter AGM

We, as graphic designers, have the ability to control to a great degree the choice of images used in the work we produce.

In the field of visual communications, our opinions are well respected and influential. I believe that with this power comes social responsibility.

It has never been more well-understood how women in our society are discriminated against. Not only are women exploited both mentally and physically; they are also subordinated economically and socially.

How design failed democracy

Fast-forward 12 years, to the turn of the millennium, when it dawned
on me that designers not only had the potential to be socially
responsible, but also may actually hold the future of the world in
their hands. Here's an example.

The most influential piece of information design in my lifetime
may very well remain the butterfly ballot used in Palm Beach
County for the November 2000 U.S. presidential election. The
number of votes mistakenly cast for independent Pat Buchanan
instead of Al Gore, due to the misleading layout, was well in excess
of George W. Bush's certified margin of victory in Florida, and
enough to result in Bush winning the presidency nationally. **The
poor design of this ballot is therefore likely responsible for the
failure of the United States** to sign the Kyoto Accord on climate
change, the 2003 invasion of Iraq in search of weapons of mass
destruction,[7] and a long list of controversial White House decisions
during the eight years that followed.

AIGA's Design for Democracy is working with the U.S. government to clean up the ballot mess, which has compromised the
mechanics of democracy.[8] As a result of its efforts, in June 2007, the
U.S. Election Assistance Commission issued voluntary guidelines
for the effective use of design in administering federal elections.
However, in the 2008 election, its recommendations were only

"It's very easy for me to see how someone could have voted for me in the belief they voted for Al Gore."

PAT BUCHANAN[9]

reflected in the ballot design of perhaps six states. The United States continues to have thousands of different ballot designs, with varied technologies, for electing one president.[10]

Responsible government should provide voters with a consistent ballot, designed by information design experts. In Canada, as in most Western democracies (let alone in countries like Afghanistan and Iraq, which ironically provide their citizens clearer ballots than the U.S. does), anything other than a professional and consistent national ballot design would be an affront. It is oddly inconsistent that, by law, the United States Food and Drug Administration requires consistent nutrition facts on every one of thousands of food package designs, while the U.S. government fails to legislate the use of a consistent, well-designed ballot and voting procedures across its 51 states and districts.

South Africa got it right the first time, in their 1994 election. The vast majority had not voted before, with a substantial portion illiterate. A simple ballot including candidate photos worked well.

The influence of design on election outcomes does not stop at the ballot box. Candidates spend most of their war chests on ads. Many of these messages are oversimplified and intentionally misleading, cunningly combining pictures and words out of context. *Advertising Age* columnist Bob Garfield admits "Political advertising is a stain on our democracy. It's the artful assembling of nominal facts into hideous, outrageous lies."[11] In 2004, U.S. presidential candidates spent over a billion dollars[12] disingenuously manipulating opinions, rather than simply presenting straightforward information that helps voters make an intelligent choice. President Obama was the third-largest advertiser in the country during the 2008 campaign,[13] including an unprecedented online effort focused on positive messages.

Palm Beach County ballot, Florida, 2000: even Pat Buchanan was shocked at his proportion of the Jewish and black vote. With many pages of voting (11 offices, 9 judicial contests, and 4 referenda) to complete, many voters wrongly marked the second hole from the top to indicate their "Democratic" intention.

PHOTO: INDIANAPOLIS STAR

Not the solution: it was just as difficult to vote for George W. Bush for president in Ohio in 2004.[14] Voting for Kerry was easy: mark box 6. But how do you vote for President Bush?

One of many sample ballots created by AIGA's Design For Democracy for the U.S. Election Assistance Commission. Their recommendations were reflected in ballot design used for the November 2008 presidential election within at least 6 states.

PHOTO COURTESY AIGA

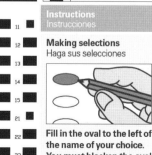

How have these manipulations become the norm? If the American public is to be equipped to choose the best leaders, we either need mandatory media literacy education starting in elementary school, or **legislation that prohibits lying with imagery as strongly as current legislation prohibits lying with words.** Meanwhile, good design can encourage youth to seize the cynical 54 percent U.S. election turnout rate as an opportunity.[15]

"Drink Milk. Love Life."

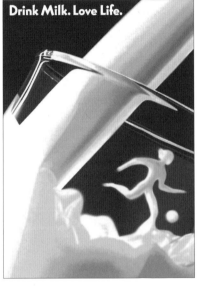

That same chad-hanging election year, my daughter Hannah and I were on the way to her school. She was eight (and a half!) years old. As we passed by a beautiful billboard that proclaimed "Drink Milk. Love Life," Hannah, who does not like drinking cow's milk, had questions.

HANNAH: "David, I don't drink that milk. Does that mean I can't love life?" [Yes, she's always called me David.]

DAVID: "No, of course not."

HANNAH: "Do I love life less than kids who drink a lot of milk?"

DAVID: "No, Hannah, they just made that up to try to convince you to drink more milk."

HANNAH (after a long pause): "Why are they allowed to say that if it isn't true?"

> ## "We do not inherit this land from our ancestors, we borrow it from our children." HAIDA PROVERB

persuasion

Good question, Hannah. At the time, I was preparing to speak at a design conference in Vancouver. Like most designers, I had planned to show my best work. But in that moment with my daughter, an idea hit me: instead of speaking about my own design work, why not instead speak about the influence of *all* design work?

What could become possible if designers used their power to influence choices and beliefs in a positive and sustainable way? **Imagine: what if we didn't just do good design... we did good?**

Many conferences, keynotes, and seminars later, I'm still traveling with that message. On the way, I've learned as much as I've taught, most often from those who are younger.

I met a young boy in rural Tanzania. He was clutching a plastic bag, decorated with the Camel cigarette brand, the only camel he is likely to meet in his lifetime.

PHOTO: DAVID BERMAN

Tengeru, Tanzania

Cuba was an unlikely place to meet American Alan Jacobson. In 2005, Alan traveled 6,000 miles to work with artist Lily Yeh's Rwanda Healing Project. There, he led the transformation of Survivors Village and The Genocide Memorial Park honoring genocide victims from the Rugerero area, where over 800,000 people were slaughtered within 100 days in 1994. "Some designers feel that there is no meaning in what they do. I hope I can inspire some to find the good to be done."

In 2002, I spoke at a design conference in Amman, Jordan. We took a day trip to Petra – an ancient city majestically carved entirely from the surface of rock, and certainly the eighth wonder of the world. There I met a young woman and her camel. They live in the nearby town of Wadi Musa, where the largest sign in the town proclaims the "Superior American Taste" of a local cigarette brand.

PHOTOS: DAVID BERMAN

Bedouin friend, Petra, Jordan. (The cat is my traveling companion, Spice, one half of twins: Blackie stays home with my daughter)

Wadi Musa, Jordan

On the flip side of my world, back home in Canada, my daughter has never seen a cigarette billboard: all tobacco advertising likely to be viewed by children is illegal in Canada.[16]

Cigarettes are among the most highly advertised products in the world. Big Tobacco spends over $13 billion a year[17] promoting their cleverly designed disposable nicotine-delivery system. Their goal: to convince all three of these youth to start smoking cigarettes, within their teenage years, until they die.

PHOTO: GEIERUNITED

The cigarette: highly effective British industrial design from the 1880s

[All $ in the book are U.S. dollars.]

In proudly free Western societies, we like to tell parents that it's up to them to control what their kids see and don't see. It is said that it takes a village to raise a child. I would add that it takes a society to raise a generation. Striving to be a good parent, I will help my daughter make clever choices around tobacco, and hope that she will live a long and healthy life, perhaps well into the next century.

When that 22nd century arrives, and our children's grandchildren look back on these remarkable days in which we lived, what will history recall as our most crucial issue?

PHOTO: HANNAH LANGFORD BERMAN

My daughter, Hannah

A teenage civilization

The potential impact of any global threat to humanity is far greater when combined with the current trend toward homogeneity of civilization design. Let me explain.

Human civilizations have come and gone, risen and fallen. Although most scientists believe our species has been around for at least five million years, this approach to social organization is only around 6,000 years old (10,000 at most).[18] However, as science philosopher Ronald Wright points out, after 6,000 years of experimenting with civilization design, we humans now find ourselves sailing together into the future on the one huge remaining ship of a combined global civilization.[19] Whether or not we welcome the idea of globalization, we are witnessing in our lifetimes our evolution into a singular, merged human community – the largest ever. There are no more geographic New Worlds to discover: only a shared destiny.

Wright goes on to describe civilization as God having let loose a special group of primates – the human animal – into the laboratory of life, giving them the power to tinker with life itself. What scares me the most about this image is that we are all now living inside the experiment: if we accidentally destroy "the lab," we have no home left, either for ourselves or our future generations.

For good or for bad, our globalized inventiveness is fusing our destinies into one civilization. So together, humanity must choose wisely, and in this lifetime. Our common future is our common design challenge.

With or without us, evolution moves forward by trial and error. But if the future is to include a recognizable human civilization, we cannot absorb one more major miscue.

I hope that, 100,000 years from now, our descendants will look back on those first 6,000 "childhood" years of the Big Bang of civilization as the successful adolescence of humanity: that awkward time when there were many civilizations would be a distant memory. Maybe we will be remembered for somehow overcoming our adolescent delusions of immortality and inane infighting, bringing forward the best of all cultures, and designing a sustainable future together: that we found a way to meet our needs without compromising the ease for future generations to meet theirs.

Wright's ship analogy describes our situation well. Consider that many miles of open sea are needed to turn a huge ship around: In the event that an iceberg appears on our horizon, we must start changing direction far in advance to avoid crashing into it. If we wait too long, we pass the event horizon, with no choice but to resign ourselves to witnessing our demise in painfully slow motion. **Design has the potential to help steer us to a safer course.**

FROM CHARLATAN ARCHIVE (SEE NOTE 20)

"As Homo sapiens' entry in any intergalactic design competition, industrial civilization would be tossed out at the qualifying round." DAVID ORR[21]

Which future should we choose?

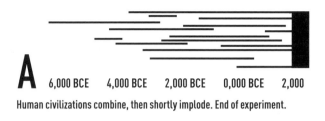

A 6,000 BCE   4,000 BCE   2,000 BCE   0,000 BCE   2,000

Human civilizations combine, then shortly implode. End of experiment.

B 6,000 BCE   4,000 BCE   2,000 BCE   0,000 BCE   2,000   4,000   6,000   8,0

Human civilizations combine, work it out, proceed with long sustainable future.

So which iceberg threatens us the most?

Is it terrorism? I don't think so. Though timely and freshly horrible in our minds, terrorism is not a new phenomenon and has yet to pose a serious threat to civilization. (I *do* think it is worth pondering why intelligent, and not particularly radical, people

Italy's Diesel brand presents a bizarre juxtaposition of Asian poverty and American poverty

from around the world are increasingly angry at and offended by Western culture. Perhaps they are outraged about being lied to continually by the most sophisticated deception process in history. More on this later.)

Perhaps the iceberg is a pandemic. A global pandemic is a highly probable catastrophe that deserves attention, including well-designed messaging to mitigate its effects. The spread of infectious disease is not new. In today's world, infectious diseases spread farther and faster than before, due to international travel

)	12,000	14,000	16,000	18,000	20,000	22,000	24,000	26,000	28,000

and shipping. The likelihood of a global pandemic of deadly, drug-resistant influenza or tuberculosis grows every day. Health authorities tell us that the question is not if, but when. Nonetheless, the worst scenario, while devastating, wouldn't likely end civilization as we know it.

Is the iceberg financial collapse? Or corruption? We'll consider design's role in these ills in the next chapter; however, we have overcome this type of challenge in the past and we will again.

No, the answer is "none of the above." When our children's children look back at the biggest issue of our era, they will see the most deadly threat as the devastation we wrought on our physical environment.

It is unfortunate that the culture that was the most influential of the 20th century also happens to be perhaps the world's most environmentally unsustainable.

> ## "There are no passengers on Spaceship Earth. We are all crew."
> ### HERBERT "MARSHALL" MCLUHAN (1911–1980)[22]

Daily News

1,200,000,000	doses of Coca-Cola ingested [23]
882,000,000	Marlboro cigarettes shipped outside the U.S. [24]
41,000,000	McDonald's customers served [25]
14,000,000	BIC pens disposed [26]
6,200,000	kilos of plastic molded for bottled water [27]
43,000	hectares of ancient forest destroyed [28]
26,500	human children under the age of 5 slain by poverty [29]
7,400	humans infected with HIV virus [30]
3,000	promotional messages seen by average American [31]
2,800	African children killed by untreated malaria [32]
600	reported deaths in car accidents in China [33]
160	HIV babies born in South Africa [34]
73	species made extinct [35]

Sudden events dominate the news, while ongoing crises fester: another day on Spaceship Earth

"Human population multiplied by aspirations for a middle-class existence divided by current technology is putting unsustainable strains on our planet."

ROBERT SHAPIRO, CEO, MONSANTO CORPORATION

2 BEYOND GREEN: A CONVENIENT LIE

TWENTY YEARS AGO, Canada's most celebrated environmentalist, David Suzuki, explained to me that among all the amazing news being reported, the single largest story of our time is that humans have gained the ability to change the physical, geological, and atmospheric nature of planet Earth. What took 4 billion years to build, we are transforming, perhaps irrevocably, in just the last 400 years. In fact, people consumed more goods and services in the second half of the 20th century than in all previous generations put together.[36]

It was May 2000 when I began speaking at design conferences about the role of designers in irrevocably damaging our planet. Back then, I would spend my first 15 minutes making the case that environmental degradation, rather than a pandemic or a meteor from deep space, was the largest threat to humanity. Starting in September 2001, with New York mayor Rudy Giuliani urging Americans that his

PHOTO: ALTON THOMPSON

Taipei 101, briefly the world's tallest skyscraper. Seismic activity in Taipei in the form of microearthquakes has increased significantly since construction began in 1997. It's believed to be due to the piling of 700,000 tons of material in one spot.[37]

battered city needed "the best shoppers in the world" and President George W. Bush telling Americans to go shopping [38] to fight terrorism, it became more difficult to keep distracted audiences' focus upon the daily realities about which we've become complacent.

A decade after that attack on the United States, mainstream news media and Web sites overflow with greener this and greener that, both in advertising and editorial. What does not get talked about enough are the root causes of environmental decay. **Why are we consuming so much?** Why are we consuming this and not that? The largest threats to our world today are rooted in over-consumption, spurred on by rapid advances in the psychology, speed, sophistication, and reach of communications technology. **Designers are at the core of the most efficient, most destructive pattern of deception in human history.**

The United States of America is a world leader in teaching the dysfunctional practice of consuming more than we need. With Americans renting over 1.8 billion square feet of storage space outside

Contrast this shoe ad to America's messages to its consumers during the Second World War.

TOMMY ☰ HILFIGER
underwear

For some, 9/11 was just another reason to sell more stuff, and companies that produce nothing but image had little difficulty finding a way to turn a profit on jingoism.

their homes,[39] and almost a third of Americans storing an obese amount of extra mass on their bodies,[40] the biggest threat to our world's environment is not the Port of New York's largest export being waste paper[41] (much of it on barges headed for Antarctica); rather it is the export of an idea.

The idea involves, as William Wordsworth described it, a society focused on getting and spending. We have an unsustainable addiction to the consumption of stuff. In a vicious circle, the North American habit of living out of balance is perpetuated by addicting other peoples and cultures. The biggest pushers are multinational corporations. And it's a pyramid scheme because the perpetrators hide the fact that we will run out of planet before everyone has achieved the desired lifestyle.

Subprime ethics

Like all pyramid scams, it is not a matter of *if* it will crash, but *when*. In 2008, to the detriment of everyone on the planet, the U.S. found itself exporting a financial crisis when the "when" arrived for the American lending market. The effects of an unprecedented level of mass greed among short-sighted lenders finally came home to millions of Americans. What initially appeared to be only a subprime mortgage crisis eventually revealed a case of subprime ethics pervading the entire lending infrastructure. And the sudden surge in U.S. homeowner debt did not rise spontaneously from some contagious bacteria infecting the brains of America's workers; it began in meticulously and strategically crafted viral ad campaigns designed to persuade people to live beyond their means.

Consider Citicorp's $1 billion award-winning[42] media campaign from 2001 to 2006 pushing second mortgages, which urged homeowners to take debt less seriously and borrow against their homes at high interest rates. The campaign used enticing visualizations of how their lives could look, combined with slogans such as "There's got to be at least $25,000 hidden in your house. We can help you find it." This traditional "last resort" form of borrowing, formerly associated with shame and the title "second mortgage," was rebranded as clever "home equity financial planning": a way to afford beautifully illustrated family vacations, shiny new SUVs, and colorful shopping sprees. The result was a thousand-fold increase in total U.S. home equity loans when compared to the early 1980s.

Ameriquest Mortgage Company splurged $2.5 million for their 30 seconds of "Don't judge too quickly... we won't" Super Bowl fame in 2004.[43] Ameriquest has since declared bankruptcy, walking away from its own debt as a record number of Americans are forced to walk away from their homes. In October 2008 alone, one in every 452 U.S. households received a foreclosure notice, as 84,000 properties were repossessed nationwide.[44]

The U.S. mortgage crisis is an example of a larger problem: overconsumption induced by irresponsible marketing inflates crises that endanger us all when the bubble bursts. I'm not speaking of an investment bubble such as we saw in the dot-com meltdown; but rather what futurist Tim O'Reilly (who coined the term "Web 2.0") refers to as a reality bubble.[45] When the gap between how things really are and how things appear (the relentless illusion painted by an industry tirelessly eager to twist our behaviors) becomes wide enough, we must endure occasional and painful seismic corrections. There is no question that award-winning advertising designs are clever and even strategic in the short term. But a free market system runs most efficiently on freely flowing information, not mass deception and trickery.

OK. But what does this alarmist rant have to do with design?

Designing climate change

There is strong scientific consensus that human activities are changing the Earth's climate, that the Earth is getting warmer because of us, and that the warming is becoming increasingly harmful.[46] And yet, industries threatened by environmental improvement spend millions promoting contrarians and disinformation to muddle the public opinion required to choose sustainability. Today, I no longer have to prove the case for the environment: I'll leave that responsibility to Al Gore and David Suzuki, should you remain unconvinced that we are in the midst of a fundamental crisis. However, I would like to spotlight the urgency to design a better way, while our fate is still within our control.

Overconsumption is the leading driver toward an environmental shipwreck. Most to blame are those in the Western World simultaneously consuming the most per capita, while convincing the larger, faster-growing populations of the Developing World to consume more and more.

The most powerful weapon we've invented to convince new markets to consume more stuff is brand advertising. It's cheaper to stretch an existing brand than to invent a better product: each year, 95 percent of the 16,000 new American brands are actually extensions of existing ones.[47] Professional communicators are the people who proudly think up clever visual persuasions intended to trigger deep emotional needs to increase

"It isn't pollution that's harming our environment: it's the impurities in our air and water." GEORGE W. BUSH

DOING GOOD The Aspen Design Challenge is an annual call that invites students worldwide to address a crucial international problem. The first was "Designing Water's Future" and challenged cross-disciplinary student teams to develop design solutions that encourage responsible water use and awareness of the importance of water conservation. It's a joint project of AIGA in the United States and INDEX in Denmark. AIGA is amongst the growing group of leaders in the design industry, who, through initiatives such as proclaiming "carbon-neutral design" are influencing designers, manufacturers, and corporate consumers to rethink design.

GO GREEN!

Eliminate unwanted paperwork by switching to our new electronic billing option for your Ottawa Citizen subscription. Sign up today to receive your subscription renewal notice instantly via email!

GO online at www.ottawacitizen.com/ebilling to make the switch or call us at 613-596-1950 or 1-800-267-6100.

easy.
convenient.
environmentally friendly.
ebilling.

OTTAWA ▲ CITIZEN

OTTAWA CITIZEN, AUGUST 28, 2008

Greenwashing 101: For many days, my local newspaper printed 150,000 copies of this quarter-page ad, urging those readers who subscribe to "go green" by choosing electronic billing: avoiding two sheets of paper a year. Over 100 pages of shopping flyers accompanied most of the issues.

consumption. Meanwhile, product designers ingeniously develop more and more stuff, and clever new processes to increase production.

Some consumption is normal and fun. However, overconsumption is a learned addiction that will not be fixed solely by "greening" every process and product: we have to stop finding clever ways of convincing each other to pick up this bad habit.

The environment is the biggest issue of the day, and the single greatest force perpetuating environmental decline is the collateral damage caused by the drive toward worldwide overconsumption. It is that simple: **humans consuming too much stuff are causing us to tear at the earth, upset the oceans, melt the poles, and litter our sky.** And the more people who buy in, the worse it becomes. We're running out of space and we have no off-site backup. The future of all that humankind has accomplished since the invention of civilization hinges upon the wisdom we show in our lifetimes.

So, will we make the choice now to continue to indulge in the proud, unbounded expression and consumption of design, or will we take up our role in helping to design a better future for all?

"Designers make the world's most beautiful trash."

SCOTT EWEN, ÉMIGRÉ

Design matters: design for all

In 2003, Steven Rosenberg (a cofounder of the Graphic Designers of Canada's Social Action Committee in the 1990s), convinced me that if ~~dolphins~~ *cats* had thumbs they would rule the world. But since they

PHOTO: JENNIFER GROEN, INNERQUEST DOLPHIN RETREATS

can't grip a pen, they can't draw pictures or write stuff down. That inability to record information forces the species to freshly reinvent their history in every generation.

Humankind's dominion over the Earth is due to our species' unique gifts: our innate mastery of language and our ability to record it. These qualities allow us to share information over great distances and across generations. We imagine the future, designing civilization on the shoulders of those who came before us.

Professional communicators and designers have stewardship of the huge responsibility that accompanies these gifts, and we have much to be proud of.

For those humans who can't grip a pen, we invent tools that remedy this challenge. The girl pictured on this page is using technology designed for quadriplegics. A person without the use of their arms or legs can surf the Internet by combining neck movements with sipping or puffing air through a tube.

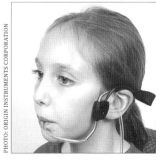

PHOTO: ORIGIN INSTRUMENTS CORPORATION

Such innovations represent perhaps the greatest liberation in human history. In the past 50 years, more people with disabilities and difficulties have been liberated from marginalized lives by technology and design than the number liberated by any revolution or war.[48]

When the idea of cutting an angle in the curb at street corners was first proposed to help people in wheelchairs, the cost was widely considered extravagant, as so few people in wheelchairs were in the streets. However once curb cuts were in place, more wheelchairs turned out to use them. A market for ruggedized electric wheelchairs emerged, and the ramps are now appreciated by anyone who has ever had to drag their luggage onto the subway.

Time and again, **designing for the extremes results in benefits for all**. In 1886, after having trouble remembering things in school, Herman Hollerith designed punched cards to help compensate for his cognitive processing deficit. At that same time, the u.s. Census Bureau was struggling to comply with the u.s. Constitution's requirement that a census be taken every 10 years. Hand counting the growing number of Americans would take more than a decade to finish! So they turned to Hollerith's punch cards for help. His Tabulating Machine Company would later be rebranded IBM.

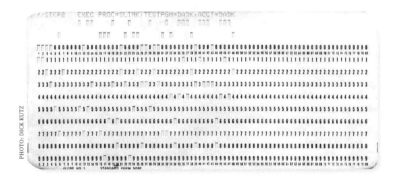

PHOTO: DICK KUTZ

Here's another case of how accommodating disabilities and difficulties can help everyone. In 1948, three Bell Labs scientists in New Jersey sought to build a hearing aid that would be less conspicuous, cheaper, and consume less power. They created the transistor. A Japanese company, now Sony, licensed the technology for $25,000 and invented the transistor radio. Later the transistor was essential to putting people on the moon and computers in our pockets.

"Over the next 10 to 15 years, technology has the capacity to virtually eliminate barriers faced by people with disabilities in the workplace." STEVE BALLMER, MICROSOFT

Vinton Cerf, the "father of the Internet," has been with Google since 2005. Back in 1972, he was working on the core protocols of ARPANET, the Internet's predecessor. Cerf had a hearing impairment, and his wife was deaf. It's told that he was so intrigued with the possibility of sending text messages to her through the computer network that he invented the electronic mail protocol.

The couple had unknowingly given birth to the Internet's "killer app." The resulting proliferation of the Web has transformed the delivery of most content to a medium that can easily be designed to transcend visual, auditory, dexterity, and cognitive impairments.

Brainchild: beyond DNA, beyond instinct

We live in a post-Darwinian world where the human species has all but stopped evolving genetically, due to advances in medicine, technology, and recorded knowledge. Genes that would tend to disappear due to "survival of the fittest" are now almost as likely to continue on, because society has become so much better at not leaving anyone behind. At the same time, we have figured out how to accelerate cultural change with mass-produced goods and mass communication. While our natural urges drive us to reproduce, our professional urges drive us to create ideas (and activate them through design and design thinking). Survival is increasingly dependent on technology, and less so on natural forces.

Indeed, we live in a time where we can easily leave a greater mark by propagating our ideas than by propagating our genetic material. Though so much human activity is driven by the instinct to reproduce our personal DNA, we can now pass on a more influential legacy by designing an idea and sharing it with millions, whether through mass production or the reach afforded by information technology such as Vint Cerf's brainchild.

PHOTO: DAVID BEERMAN

Assorted ebony carvings displayed in market gift shop in Serengeti, Tanzania

> **"A journey of a thousand miles begins with one small step."** CONFUCIUS

3 POP LANDSCAPE

THE MOST UNDERSTOOD WORD, no matter where you go in the world, is *OK*. The second most understood word is *Coke*.[49] And 1.2 billion times a day, someone reaches for one.[50]

coke

The patron saint of seasonal overconsumption has replaced the spiritual focus of Christmas with a festival of marketing, materialism, the accompanying waste... and stress of compliance

As intended by The Coca-Cola Company's first president, Asa Griggs Candler,[51] we find the world's most-recognized product within easy reach all over the globe. Coca-Cola is famous for a string of marketing firsts. Its creative team reinvented a Christian saint as a North American marketing mascot, and were the first to use pictures of women to systematically sell stuff on a massive scale.

On the streets of my hometown of Ottawa, the six-foot, backlit, all-weather, refrigerated billboards we call Coke machines have become commonplace. I am told by a manager at our local bottler that they operate at a loss as often as at a profit. These drink dispensers beckon from the sidewalks outside our corner stores in the summer heat, while our city suffers from rotating power brownouts.

Other entrepreneurs have learned from Coke: A few years ago, a company offered to put recycling bins and park benches around Canada's capital, at no apparent cost to our city. The cash-strapped municipal government embraced the idea. Now we enjoy advertising shaped into thin recycling bins all over town, or

PHOTOS: DAVID BERMAN

As in most of Earth's urban spaces, advertising is taking over the streets of my hometown

posing as garbage cans, each with a park bench attached. One such recycling station is planted on a traffic island where one must cross traffic on foot (or toss your recyclables from a moving car) to use the bin. The view when seated on many of the benches is four to six lanes of cars and trucks, while ads for products such as soft drinks are in plain view when sitting gridlocked in traffic.

Coke has gone far further. The most remote journey I've ever taken was mountain trekking high above Tanzania. At the last outpost en route to the 4,600-meter peak, after two days of climbing and camping with fellow travelers Paul and Spice,[52] I discovered that someone had soldiered ahead to ensure I could exchange 10,000 Tanzanian shillings for "the pause that refreshes!"

PHOTOS: DAVID BERMAN

Refreshments for sale at Saddle Hut, altitude 3,570 meters. The Kilimanjaro water brand is also owned by The Coca-Cola Company.[53]

DOING GOOD

The first time we met, Seoul's Don Ryun Chang kindly corrected my claim that Canada had the world's highest proportion of high-speed Internet connected citizens: that honor now belongs to South Korea. As Icograda's president, Don insisted that his tireless crisscrossing of the planet is not entirely selfless — boosting the awareness of Asian presence in the design world also helps his personal design agenda. "Design is the universal equalizer. When done effectively and with integrity, it provides aesthetic, economic, social, and cultural value."

I thought this would be the extent of Coke's admirable branding reach. Fatigued and exhilarated after making our descent, we headed overland toward the airport in Arusha, Tanzania's second-largest city. Crossing the countryside, we saw respected schools, orphanages, and hospitals, all branded with Coke signs.

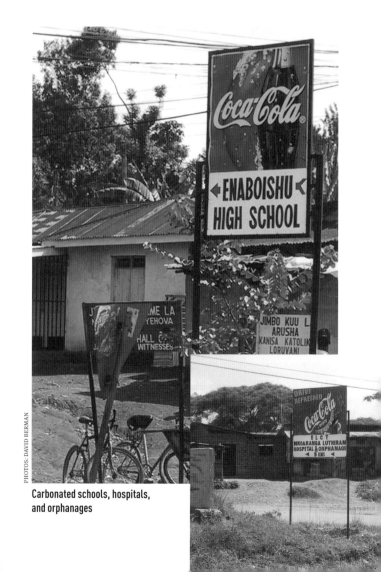

PHOTOS: DAVID BERMAN

Carbonated schools, hospitals, and orphanages

Worse yet, every village on the road to Arusha was branded with soft drink logos, as if they were North American corner stores. Later that week, Amyn Bapoo, the Aga Khan Foundation's director in Tanzania, explained to me over dinner that the annual fee to brand a village was only around $200. The villages are very proud of these brands of legitimacy; they aren't on the map without one.

PHOTO: DAVID BERMAN

Official signage, Meserani, Tanzania

Coke's coverage didn't stop with villages and schools: along the side of Tanzania's main highways, official milestones show the distance to major cities. But each milestone is also an ad: permanent cement markers sunk deep in the African earth, branded with the Coca-Cola logo.

PHOTOS: DAVID BERMAN

Official government highway distance marker to Arusha, Tanzania's second-largest city

expro

If that wasn't enough to convince me of Coca-Cola's branding conquest of Tanzania, arriving on Tanzania's island of Zanzibar added more fizz. I discovered this wonderful ancient town of mystery, scent, and enchantment now brandishing Coke ads as the official street signs on every corner.

PHOTOS: DAVID BERMAN

priation

DOING GOOD

David Stairs had been coordinating the graphic design program at Central Michigan University for over six years when he launched Designers Without Borders in Kampala in December 2000 in response to the needs of one under-resourced school in Uganda. This grassroots non-profit organization was the first in the world with a mission to enhance development through communication design education. Today, DWB delivers equipment, instruction, and design consulting to schools and select non-profits in many parts of Africa.

During the 1990s, while Tanzania was challenged with disease, corruption, and poverty,[54] Coca-Cola offered to take care of their road signage and, despite the occasional Pepsi sign, turned Tanzania into a Coke country.

It's masterful branding. There is much marketing savvy to learn from Coca-Cola's advertising quest to become the most recognized product brand on Earth, as well as its Santa Claus parade of marketing firsts. Ingenious. Clever. But wise?

Tanzania, a country of 40 million,[55] has epidemic malaria, which either kills or debilitates those who suffer from it. With approximately 16 million cases annually, 80,000 children under the age of five die each year.[56]

Consider that in some parts of Africa, Coca-Cola is considered medicinal.[57] And on the desperately poor Tanzanian streets,[58] the price of a bottle of Coke is about

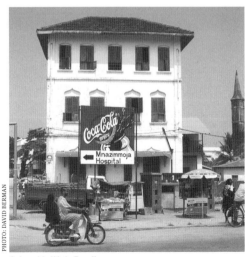

PHOTO: DAVID BERMAN

Coke adds life in Zanzibar

the same as the price of an anti-malaria pill. While Coke is the best selling drink on the continent, a million Africans die each year of malaria.[59]

I am not suggesting that the West should not share with the Developing World. However we have many far better things to share than our dependence on carbonated caffeine. It's an impressive feat to convince Mexicans to drink 487 bottles of Coke a person each year.[60] **But rather than sharing our cycles of style, consumption, and chemical addictions, designers can use their professional power, persuasive skills, and wisdom to help distribute ideas that the world really needs:** health information, conflict resolution, tolerance, technology, freedom of the press, freedom of speech, human rights, democracy... as well as to share the antidote for the buying and spending virus for which all have not yet built up resistance.

Since I was first inspired by Herb Lubalin's application of typography to socially just causes, I have believed in the power of design to create awareness for the public good.

HERB LUBALIN

COURTESY OMAR VULPINARI/FABRICA

THE NEXT WAR WILL DETERMINE NOT WHAT IS RIGHT BUT WHAT IS LEFT.

CIUDAD JUA
300 MUJERES MUERTAS 500 MUJERES

Too late to fasten your seat-belt

Simon's already doing it! cdalife.org

Imagine what would be possible if The Coca-Cola Company's uncommonly efficient distribution system in Africa could be harnessed to deliver health information, medicine, and condoms, in addition to caffeinated sugar water.

Alfred Nobel invented dynamite. Albert Einstein brought to the attention of President Roosevelt the potential of the atomic bomb.[61] Both were brilliant men who probably died with heavy hearts. If they were with us today, I believe they would tell us "Be very careful with what you create."

In a well-designed future, it will be the message crafters, the product designers, and the experts in transporting ideas and artifacts across great distances and generations who may hold the greatest responsibility. We all have a duty to make sure that the inventions we embrace and enhance by design are not just clever but also wise; that we don't just create intriguing, marketable stuff, but that our creations are aligned with a sustainable future for human cultures and civilization as a whole.

COURTESY ZORAN GABRIJAN/BENJAMIN IVANĖIĖ
Translation: My mother smokes...

Usurping cultural landscape

Though sharing democracy is something North Americans often lay claim to, we erode our democratic ideals when we allow our own shared spaces to become just more marketing real estate for a passing multinational corporation's marketing plan. Something precious is lost: As we corrupt common spaces, we corrupt our common mind. Ubiquitous marketing doesn't just cost a slice of our mindshare: it also compromises the root social-democratic concept that we are all entitled to equality, though we may differ in what we own or consume.

Beijing's Forbidden City, now brought to you by American Express

COURTESY JAMES EBERHARDT

Coke is working hard to make sure you can't visit the Great Wall of China without seeing a Coke sign.

In 1960, President John F. Kennedy gave his nomination speech at the Democratic National Convention within the storied Los Angeles Memorial Coliseum, a structure named in memory of veterans of the First World War. In 2008, President Barack Obama's nominating convention took place in a building called Pepsi Center, and he gave his acceptance speech from Invesco Field, named after a Georgia-based investment firm.

Before the First World War, the only major-league sports venue in North America linked to a brand was Chicago's Wrigley Field (the chewing gum magnate owned the Cubs at the time). The next corporate branding of a sports stadium didn't appear until 1953 on St. Louis's Busch Stadium: the local Busch brewery family both owned the team and championed the construction.

PHOTO: DAVID BERMAN

The world's most famous sports brand appeased fan outrage with a compromise: in 2009, they crossed the street to the new "Yankee Stadium in [your name here] Park."

But in 1988, the historic Los Angeles Forum was renamed Great Western Forum with cold insurance company cash. Today, over 60 percent of major-league-baseball stadia have sold their identities.[62] It's an icy slope: In 1993, Disney named the Anaheim Mighty Ducks hockey franchise to promote a family film – what would Lord Stanley say? In Europe, it's now common for the largest words sported on football (soccer) jerseys to be corporate names.

It seems like pretty easy money, so why not run with it? Because it's not actually free. The cost is what economists call an externality, a cost borne by a third party beyond the direct participants in the transaction. In this case, it costs local population a loss of culture and history. Local culture is traded for homogeneity, while tax relief funds the salaries of superbrand athletes. This externality of branding buildings may seem subtle because we're used to it, so let's consider some fresher scenarios.

Would it cost you any peace of mind if, the next time you strapped into an airline seat, you looked up to discover the inside of the airplane had as many ads as a city bus? (Just in the past few years, we already see advertising seeping into video screens at every seat.) Would it be okay with you if the handle of every public drinking fountain had an ad encouraging you to down a Pepsi instead? What if every car park in your downtown banded together to sell their airspace by pimping their brands to the highest bidder: Exxon Parking? Priceline Parking? Perhaps some entrepreneur should simply start a clothing line branded with a blue sans serif *P*.

PHOTOS: DAVID BERMAN

How did we convince most of the world to use the letter *P* for parking, no matter the local language? It's certainly an uninspired piece of icon design. And how would you feel if there were symbols in a language foreign to you all over *your* town? I'm surprised it's even legal in Québec, considering that province's extreme language laws: "parking" en français begins with an *S*.

DOING GOOD Eric Karjaluoto of Vancouver's SmashLab was doing brand identity work in 2006 when he was inspired by Al Gore's *An Inconvenient Truth*. "The world was in a bad state, and I had a child on the way. We thought we should be more green, but had no idea of how to do it. It occurred to us that most designers probably didn't know how either. Social responsibility isn't the main thing we do." So they created DesignCanChange.org as a starting point for designers seeking to commit to sustainable practice. In the site's first year, designers from 77 countries signed in. "I'm always blown away when I get e-mail from people who were inspired by our site."

Many American states hold easy-to-leverage brands (think California raisins or Florida oranges), but how about the less-famous members of the union? If the aboriginal cachet is no longer pulling traffic for "North Dakota," why not just rename the state, or even trade the right to brand the entire territory to the highest corporate bidder? Imagine your new license plate from the Great State of Northwest Airlines, just a short commute from the Great State of Southwest Airlines.

From Montpelier to São Paolo

Instead, in our states, our cities, and our countries, we can choose to retain the dignity and quality of our public spaces. The State of Vermont banned all billboards in 1968, in an effort to keep the Green Mountain State visibly so. It isn't perfect: "rolling stock" (moving vehicles) is exempt from the law, and marketers still sometimes park trucks as advertisements. Ted Riehle, hero of the "Billboard Law," died on New Year's Eve 2008, just missing the 40th anniversary year of his ongoing legacy. Alaska, Maine, and Hawaii have since followed Vermont's example.

PHOTO: MATT WILLS

PHOTO: DAVID BERMAN

The standard set by Vermont's sign law has been adopted to some degree in my province. We're getting there...

2007: Twenty storey advertising in São Paolo

2008: Zero storey advertising in São Paolo

In January 2008, I witnessed the remarkable outcome of an inspiring change along the skyline of sprawling São Paolo, Brazil. The world's fourth largest metropolis used to have approximately 13,000 billboards, layered so thick that it inspired the extreme advertising portrayed in Terry Gilliam's 1985 film *Brazil*. In 2007, São Paolo completely outlawed billboard advertising.[63] Knocking down arguments that loss of lighting from outdoor advertising would make the streets less safe at night (imagine!), Brazil's largest city banned all billboards on public spaces (including the "rolling stock"– the sides of buses and taxis). This required the removal of thousands of ads by the deadline. The result: a 70 percent approval rating from the citizens.[64]

Ruth Klotzel, a member of Associação dos Designers Gráficos, which led the coalition to demand the law, told me that "the change evokes childhood memories: playing on the streets, cars and houses left unlocked, when no children were killed by random violence, where we did not feel the need for the fancy clothes and TV sets, and more than one watch. The transparent skyline reveals our history

(both kind and brutal). We no longer abdicate our personality to private interests. We have reclaimed our space and our past, and rescued our dignity."

But the larger question is this: What powerful force motivated the erection of 13,000 Portuguese billboards – mostly brand advertising – in the first place? The pollution of our physical environment is rooted in the pollution of our mental environment.

PHOTO: ROBERT L. PETERS

If only all weapons could be this clever: promotion for Belgian crime writer Pieter Aspe

PHOTO: ARTURO DE ALBORNOZ

> **"Designers: don't work for companies that want you to lie for them."** TIBOR KALMAN (1949–1999)

4 THE WEAPONS: VISUAL LIES, MANUFACTURED NEEDS

WHEN I ASK MOST PEOPLE what they think of the design of the Coca-Cola wordmark, they say "Great logo!" However, if you look at it as if you've never seen it before – as a piece of typography it is awkward to read, and crudely lettered by the inventor's bookkeeper in a Spencerian typestyle we now usually reserve for schmaltzy wedding invitations.

No, the equity and charm of the Coca-Cola mark as the world's most recognized consumer product brand is not in its graphic design,[65] but rather in its history of consistent and incessant repetition. Though you've seen it thousands of times, you'll never see it in green, nor in the wrong typeface. And though this page is black and white, you can easily close your eyes and visualize Coca-Cola red. Even in the dark, you can recognize the shape of a Coke bottle by feel. For this, The Coca-Cola Company is to be congratulated.

PHOTO: DAVID BERMAN

The corporation stands up as relatively noble when examined under the bright retail lights: the Coke brand only appears on its cola (it doesn't even appear on other soft drinks that The Coca-Cola Company produces) so the word "Coke" continues to add value to the specific product that made it famous. In stark contrast, companies like Nautica, Tommy Hilfiger, and Nike don't actually manufacture anything at all: they just brand, often recklessly so.

By the time I set up my typography studio, the art of branding had undergone a transformation. No longer just a product enhancement, branding became the commodity. The brand name itself is for sale as a representation of an ideal, a lifestyle, a philosophy. There was a time I could walk into a sporting goods store looking for my next pair of basketball shorts and find all my choices in one part of the store. Today I must travel from the Adidas substore to the Nike substore to the Reebok substore, as some far-off coven of "brand managers" crosstrains me to go brand shopping rather than shorts shopping.

> ## "I don't love it, but it'll grow on me."
> ### PHIL KNIGHT
> After paying $35 for the original Nike swoosh
> from designer Carolyn Davidson

PHOTOS : DAVID BERMAN

"Nike" yarmulke,
Ottawa, Canada

"Nike" butcher shop in
Meseranti, Tanzania

Politicians try to gain name recognition by littering our street corners during elections with signs printed only with their names. They know how much humans prefer the familiar.

We know that 60 percent of consumers prefer the comfort and security of a national brand over a no-name product or service,[66] and that preference extends to all products sold under that brand. Try on the example of Nike baseball caps. Nike made its reputation by delivering quality shoes, and built a customer base who trusted its brand. So when Nike chooses to sell baseball caps, the same group of loyal customers is ready to consume such hats because they believe that Nike would only make great products. Then Nike adds a huge Nike logo on the front of the cap. Now consumers have another reason to buy the product: they can publicly proclaim their membership in the Nike club and align themselves with a reputation of quality and style. Thus, a $4 hat becomes a $19.95 hat (plus a free walking billboard for Nike) even though Nike is not an innovator in the hat-making industry.

PHOTO: DAVID BERMAN

Choosing "Nike" product in a six-floor Beijing superstore of often-counterfeit merchandise. The near-perfect label reads: "A poreion of your purchase supports youth community…"

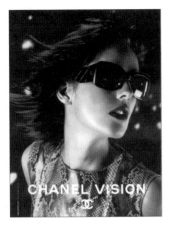

Taking advantage of the trust people naturally place in a familiar name leads many firms to put their names on products they don't actually make.

Chanel, known for classic design of dresses, takes a $5 pair of sunglasses, adds their name, and increases the retail price over 40-fold: a hefty and quick profit. Trading on its good name worked for perfume, so why not eyewear?

Hugo Boss is in on the eyewear profits too. He knew how to produce startling high-end menswear (including the masterfully intimidating SS uniforms designed with graphic designer Walter Heck, and the creation of the Hitler Youth's brown shirts[67]), but perhaps comes up short on optics.

I doubt Nautica has vision experts on staff either, but the company can see the potential for a quick buck.

So why are the big brands shocked when people are happy to discover they can just buy the symbol after all? Companies who brand indiscriminately compromise their brand equity by diluting the legitimate links to quality that their brand's legitimate value was built upon.[68]

PHOTO: DAVID BERMAN

Choosing shady sunglasses on the Embarcadero, San Francisco, California

Brand literacy

Adbusters magazine founder Kalle Lasn claims that most North Americans can only identify 10 plants, yet can recognize 1,000 corporate brands.[69] I am embarrassed to say that the birds I know best are blue jays, cardinals, and orioles, having grown up a fan of major-league baseball.[70] The average American encounters over 3,000 promotional visual messages each day (up from 560 in 1971).[71]

DOING GOOD Vancouver's Kalle Lasn launched *Adbusters* magazine in 1989, when mainstream media, such as the Canadian Broadcasting Corporation, refused to sell him airtime for his anti-logging messages. His culture-jamming magazine now has a global circulation of 100,000. Make that 100,001.

"Logos have become the closest thing we have to an international language, recognized and understood in many more places than English." NAOMI KLEIN

COURTESY CORPORATE DESIGN FOUNDATION (SEE NOTE 72)

Can you name the brands?

I'd rather learn Hangul, the best alphabet on Earth!

I showed this array of logo fragments to an audience of designers in Amman, Jordan. Each logo has had its color removed; each only shows a small part of the symbol. Even before I'd finished explaining what I've just told you, audience members correctly called out the brand names represented by 17 of the 18 logos.

The one that amazes me most is the FedEx logo. The fragment is simply the letters "Fe," in one of the world's most common typefaces. Does this mean that every time a sentence begins with "Feel" or "Feminine" or "Ferret" in a similar sans serif font, we are subconsciously reminded of what we must do if our package absolutely, positively, must get there overnight?

Ultimately, consumers pay the cost of all this advertising. The syrup in a bottle of Coke costs the bottler one-twentieth of a cent. The average cost of successfully launching a brand in the U.S. is over $30 million.[73] Meanwhile, growth in global ad spending outpaces the growth of the world economy by one-third.[74]

So how much is a message worth?

How much is space in our brains worth? Of course our brains are invaluable: perhaps the most fascinating, precious things in the universe. But in the same way that insurance actuaries must assign a cold hard cash value to a human life, can we quantify the value of a cubbyhole in the human brain? An event in the 1990s makes it possible...

In 1995, Michael Jordan wasn't playing basketball. Michael, the world's most successful superbrand, had decided to retire from the sport, after leading the Chicago Bulls to three championships in a row, to pursue his boyhood dream of becoming a baseball major-leaguer. It didn't pan out. In the 11 days between when the rumors began and Michael Jordan press-conferenced his return to basketball, the total market capitalization (total shares multiplied by the price for one share) of Michael's top five corporate endorsers (McDonald's, Sara Lee, Nike, General Mills, and Quaker) rose $3.8 billion.[75] That's the perceived worth of us all knowing of the change in Michael Jordan's career: over 50 cents for each human being on Earth.

Where is that money? It's not sitting in a bank somewhere. Instead, it represents mindshare: shares of our minds. The stock market assigned a value of over 50 cents for each brain that knew Michael was slam-dunking again above a wooden stadium floor in Chicago.

You too can smell like a basketball player

James Naismith, inventor of basketball,[76] who grew up less than 50 kilometers from my home, would have become a multimillionaire if he'd had an agent

Fast-forward to August 2008, when we witnessed China spending more than $40 billion on the Olympics, dramatically injecting the minds of television viewers worldwide with an impressively repositioned brand of the world's third-largest purchasing power. For the bargain price of around $6 a head, this form of invasion is certainly cheaper than conventional warfare ... perhaps it now is conventional warfare.

The shift for the China brand for me occurred in 2006, when my friend Professor Xiao Yong toured me through a tucked-away section of CAFA, China's top design school. There, his team of professors and students was diligently crafting the entire Beijing 2008 look: banners, medals, wayfinding signage... I was impressed to see students perfecting an identity system that could best the work of a top global design agency in London or Los Angeles. I found myself correcting negative bias I had been taught long ago against the Chinese system of governance.

PHOTO: DAVID BERMAN

Students working on the graphics for the Beijing Olympics at CAFA, 2006

In 1988, Philip Morris, desperate to further diversify its tobacco roots, bought Kraft Foods, what was then the largest non-oil acquisition in U.S. history. They paid more than $12.9 billion, three times its market valuation, due to its brand equity. The value attributed to branding changed forever.[77]

After a talk on design ethics in Oslo, I was hunting for my favorite Scandinavian snack, salt licorice. Jan Neste, president of Grafill (the Norwegian Association of Graphic Designers and Illustrators), proudly offered me a Freia Melkesjokolade chocolate bar instead. We turned over the famous yellow package and discovered that Freia was now owned by Kraft: Norway's most beloved candy brand had been bought by an American tobacco company.

Today, brand valuation falls within U.S. Generally Accepted Accounting Principles (GAAP), and there is now an ISO committee for an international standard on brand valuation.

WHY ARE YOU
BUYING YOUR FOOD
FROM A
TOBACCO COMPANY?

COURTESY ADBUSTERS

Philip Morris combined Kraft with General Foods, then added Nabisco in 2000

DOING GOOD When I met designer Zelda Harrison in Seattle, I learned that she spent her teenage years in Ghana, weathering extreme deprivation including famine. "Having to do without and be creative about finding enough to eat really makes you focus on what truly matters," she told me. "Recycling, avoiding waste and overconsumption were never an issue". Zelda now designs in Los Angeles, volunteering as head of AIGA Center for Cross-Cultural Design. The Center helps designers think beyond their national and cultural borders. For example, their Sharing Dreams program is bridging the political divide between the US and Cuba.

DOING GOOD   Earlier this year, I met Seoul mayor Oh Se-hoon, who says "Design has the power to change the world." Designated a World Design Capital, the world's second most populated metropolitan area takes design so seriously it now has a CDO – a Chief Design Officer.

Global Branding 2.0

Remember what I said about Michael Jordan and 50 cents a brain? Since only a fraction of all 6.7 billion humans are in Michael's target audience, the message value for each target brain is actually much larger. Or is it? Would it be defensible to include the entire world population in this calculation? The reach of marketing messages has grown dramatically since 1995. In 2003, the NBA sold over $600 million in merchandise outside the U.S. (that doesn't include broadcasting revenue).[78] The Internet represents the quickest proliferation of visual messages in the history of the planet. According to business guru Tom Peters, it took 37 years for radio to penetrate 15 million homes in the U.S., while the Web reached that point within four years.

Like many, I assumed the Internet would increase open competition because it lowered the cost of entering the market. And while it has created what *Wired*'s Chris Anderson calls "the long tail," where virtual bookshelves can hold far more titles than brick-and-mortars, there doesn't appear to be any less market concentration at the top.

Indeed our current era is defined by falling telecommunications costs, making it easier to promote concentration of a particular brand. The American JBANetwork e-mail service offers to send 10 million

"Whether we will acquire the understanding and wisdom to come to grips with the scientific revelations of the 20th century will be the most profound challenge of the 21st."

CARL SAGAN (1934–1996)

e-mails for $8,000, at a rate of more than 100,000 messages an hour. **Our ability to transmit information and products to new markets has never been less expensive or more immediate.** Further, the sophistication of how messages are used to influence behavior is ever-increasing, as research into the mechanics of neurology and human behavior flourishes.

The more that the Internet makes us all broadcasters, all consumers, all potential makers of things explosive, the more we need the guidance of our parents, our teachers ... our principles.

The globalization of overconsumption and lying is obviously counterproductive. Whether you are a fan of globalization or not, it is an unstoppable force. However, globalization can enable an emerging nation to progress in only 10 years to the same place that took 200 years for the United States. Such rapid development carries a correspondingly serious risk to cultural diversity. One way to protect that culture is by expressing it within principled and ethical professional behavior: such expression can help inoculate a culture from the downside of globalization's velocity.

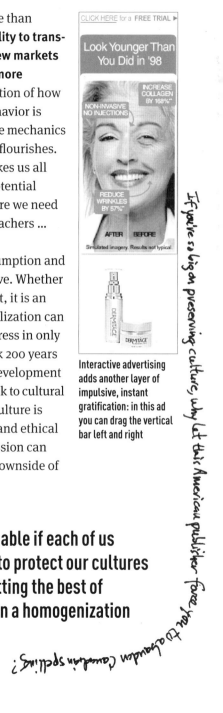

Interactive advertising adds another layer of impulsive, instant gratification: in this ad you can drag the vertical bar left and right

If you're so big on preserving culture, why let this American publisher force you to abandon Canadian spelling?

"Globalization will be sustainable if each of us manages the filters needed to protect our cultures and environments, while getting the best of everyone else's... rather than a homogenization of them." THOMAS FRIEDMAN

Willkommen in Dachau
Frauenhoferstraße

Train station, Dachau, Germany, 2006

PHOTO: DAVID BERMAN

> "What is wrong is a style of life which is presented to be better, when it is directed towards having rather than being."
>
> POPE JOHN PAUL II (1920–2005)

5 WHERE THE TRUTH LIES: A SLIPPERY SLOPE

TO PARAPHRASE STEVE MANN, the eye is the largest bandwidth pipe into the human brain, and graphic designers spend their days designing what goes in.[79] When you leverage such power in order to deceive people, then those cleverly crafted messages and images become lies. We have a responsibility to not exploit this power.

Are branding and advertising, by their very natures, misleading? Not at all. **Most advertising is truthful.** I love clever branding and advertising. Great advertising can drive down prices, support healthy competition, promote innovation, and even entertain. Advertising is part of human culture and has been helping people get information they can use to choose products, ideas, and actions ever since the first "Cave For Rent" sign went up. I'm even nostalgically charmed in discovering yet another Wall Drug sign. The drug store in Wall, South Dakota, spends around $400,000 a year on billboards that run for thousands of miles on American interstates.

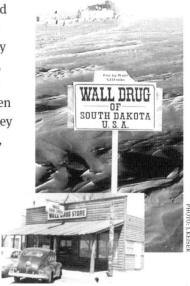

Top: Wall Drug sign at the South Pole: free ice water, just 9,333 miles
Bottom: Wall Drug Store, 1949

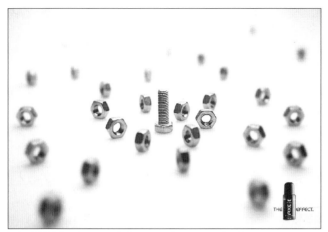

Beirut's Walid Azzi presented this clever ad as an example of how to promote a sexy product using imagery in a sophisticated way. As publisher of *ArabAd*, the Arab world's largest industry journal, he knows his audience: we were in a conference hall in Bahrain, where culture forbids exploitative images of women.

A picture can speak louder than words, and thoughts completed by the viewer will often linger longer than those that are spelled out.

As of 2005, the Red Cross is now augmented by the Red Crystal, allowing all major faiths to participate.

Certification of the International Wool Secretariat, designed by Francesco Seraglio in 1964

The Morton Salt girl

800 to 3,000 percent markup

There exist wonderful examples of effective and positive branding of worthwhile organizations, products, and ideas. Since 1863, international brands such as the Red Cross have served society: everywhere you go, people know they can run to such humanitarian symbols when they need help, food, or emergency shelter.

The Woolmark is a very useful brand: it tells me that the jacket I'm thinking to buy is made of wool, and guaranteed to a certain level of quality.

Morton Salt's delightfully clever slogan distinguishes its product as the one that will pour even when humidity is high. Clear, helpful, and memorable.[80]

Orville Redenbacher took the commodity of popping corn, which costs little to produce, and found success in the huge gap between the cost of the product and the perceived value in making it pop slightly larger. I have no qualms with him figuring out how to earn over a 1,000 percent markup while encouraging us all to consume more fiber. But was Orville dreamed up by some clever ad agency? No: Orville really existed. Born in Indiana in 1907, he grew his first corn at 12 and it put him through college. Later he developed light and fluffy hybrids, before peacefully popping off in his Jacuzzi in 1995.

Now consider a bottle of the world's top-selling liquor.[81] How old do you figure the Baileys Original Irish Cream recipe is? The Celtic imagery of the label gives the sense of a tradition going back perhaps hundreds of years.

In truth, the Baileys recipe was invented in a London boardroom in 1974, when a glut on the Irish milk market ran up against the puzzle of how to get young women to drink 80-proof whiskey.[82] The Baileys "family name" was taken from a hotel visible from the office window. Today, the Baileys myth is sold in over 130 countries. The milk used in Baileys accounts for over four percent of Ireland's total milk production.

PHOTO: DAVID BERMAN

So what's wrong with weaving powerful messaging and branding?

Marketers often seek ways of engaging their audiences on a deeply subconscious level, by linking invented images with trusted reference points in their audience's memories.

THE MILK OF IRELAND

Today, the Baileys myth is sold in over 130 countries.

How powerful is this kind of activity? Bruce Brown, a brilliant Scottish design professor, currently pro-vice chancellor at University of Brighton, taught me to think of graphic design as "designing memories."[83] Newsprint may only carry an advertisement for 24 hours before it lands in the recycling bin; however, if the designer has succeeded, the images and ideas conveyed linger in our minds, lurking, waiting to leap into our consciousness when the correct mix of desire and opportunity intersect.

As psychologist Howard Gardner points out, the basic unit of human thought is the symbol. Of all the animals, humans are the symbol-makers. Many symbols (and remember that words are also symbols) are designed to deceive as well as to inform. Symbols are the building blocks of reason and of memory, so it is unethical to intentionally insert misleading symbols ... and cruel, as our memories retain such symbols long past the point that we have classified their intended meanings as unreasonable. It is also well understood that people expose themselves selectively to facts that don't support their first impressions.

Our ability to recognize and trust symbols can be a matter of life and death – ask any color-blind driver approaching a red traffic signal. And we are naturally inclined to trust all images, because until very recently in the long history of animals, the only untrustable images were in puddles and mirages.

Designing memories

So how persistent are the memories created by brand advertising? Here's a powerful example of the extent to which images can linger. In 1981, a false rumor surfaced linking Procter & Gamble's trademark logo to Satanism.

After four years of frustration trying to quell the rumor, the corporation removed the symbol from all packaging. Five years further along, in 1990, Procter & Gamble was still receiving 350 calls a day asking about the logo's demonic past.[84]

Procter & Gamble logo, pre-1985

DOING GOOD Five minutes into our first meeting, Russell Kennedy and I were already swapping strategies about working to promote aboriginal culture in Canada and Australia. Russell was a lecturer at Melbourne's Monash University researching national identity and flag design in Australia. He was struck by the lack of acknowledgement of aboriginal culture within Australia's national identity and realized that the same challenge existed for indigenous culture on every continent. The result: INDIGO, a global network of local and indigenous designers to practice, promote, and explore indigenous design – not just as history, but as living evolving culture. In 20008, Russell was president-elect of Icograda: "Like journalists, novelists and filmmakers, designers have the ability to drive the social agenda rather than respond to it."

Here's a more unsettling example of the persistence and influence of manufactured memories:

Tragically, the Nazi party and its use of the swastika represents perhaps the most effective branding campaign of the 20th century.

Hitler's party repurposed this famous symbol. The swastika has been used for thousands of years by various cultures. (Sadly, none of them chose to trademark it).

Though this simple arrangement of the two crossed squiggles represents a regime that met its demise in the 1940s, its ability to make many in Western culture wince persists today. A symbol that meant little in the West a hundred years ago was permanently infused with ample meaning by an intentional exercise in identity branding and association.

PHOTOS: DAVID BERMAN

Sukuram Temple path lighting, South Korea   Storefront, Beijing, China

So what is the potential power, destructive or otherwise, of the memorized symbols and the ideas associated with them that are left behind in people's brains? The 20th century was driven by this persuasiveness of ideas, which resulted in the quickest, most widespread torrent of murder and social upheaval in the history of civilization.[85]

How many died in the past 100 years due to buildings collapsing? Compare that to the tens of millions murdered in the same period due to the carefully orchestrated propagation and perpetuation of evil lies.

Today, in the Developed World, we insist that a certified architect approve plans for all commercial buildings. This is wise: as a society, we recognize the potential danger if buildings like the one you may be in right now falls down. I believe the time will soon come when our civilization matures enough to recognize that visual communicators manufacture misleading memories, and those visual lies can be just as dangerous as melted steel.

Except the most powerful, largest lying machines in the world today are not the Nazis or any other political party. Nor is it Al-Qaeda.

In Canada, you only need to take 0.5 percent of the beer market to have a successful brand.[86] You can choose to design packaging that repels most, yet as long as it appeals to a niche it will succeed. So what stops a designer from helping a microbrewery put a swastika on a beer label, knowing that they could sell over 0.5 percent on shock value alone? (Clearly the example is extreme, however our globalized wine stores now sell imported labels with names such as "Fat Bastard" and "Cat's Pee," which use a calmer version of the same mechanism.)

Whether the lingering visual memories are the sexuality of Internet pornography or the idealized images of beauty that convince Colombian 14-year-old girls to ask for breast implant surgery for their quinceaños (the traditional Catholic 15th birthday coming-of-age party)[87] – whether it's Brazilian peasant women in Amazonia buying Avon cosmetics rather than food[88] or the violence of Saturday morning cartoons – the design of memorable imagery is powerful weaponry.

The same symbolism can be used as a force of good: swastikas in this ad by anti-Nazi group Exit attract neo-Nazi youth to Exit's strategy that helps European kids out of a maze of hate.

Where does the answer lie?

The answer lies in where we will draw the line of what is acceptable, and how soon. If the market is left to draw the line, then the integrity of the design professions will also likely be called into question (and rightfully so). Better that the professionals establish a higher standard than what prevailing social morality will tolerate.

Who gives permission to a soy milk advertiser to use one of the most sacred symbols of Eastern religion to have us change our breakfast habits? There is an irony when large corporations, typically the biggest fans of trademark law, rip off the meaning of a symbol that has been built up over thousands of years of cultural activity.

I wonder if it would be different if a Christian cross was used to sell cereal. How long until someone recognizes the power and potential leverage of that symbol? Perhaps someone already has.

TASTE AND NUTRITION CO-HABITATE HARMONIOUSLY.

GET YOUR SOY WITH SILK.

Selling soy milk by selling out the sacred

DOING GOOD

Design has the sense and persuasiveness to cross challenging borders. I first came across Halim Choueiry, then from the Lebanese American University, in a restaurant full of designers in Brno, Czech Republic. He was exchanging design education strategies with designers from a surprising variety of countries. Halim is now a professor in Doha, encouraging Qatari women to embrace careers in communication design. As he puts it, "No matter what beliefs we each hold about who created our universe or how, we cannot deny that he or she or it is a fantastic designer. Sometimes it feels like we are setting out to destroy this great design, forgetting that we are all an essential part of it."

In the midst of the riot (and more than 100 deaths) around the publishing of cartoons depicting the prophet Muhammad in a Danish newspaper, I was asked by a Canadian reporter if I thought *Jyllands-Posten* had the right to publish those drawings. My response was that they certainly did.[89] But I added this: just because we can do something, doesn't mean we should. And that is where professional judgment is needed. "Do no harm" is an excellent signpost.

CHICKEN DELIGHT DINE-IN TAKE OUT

PHOTO: DAVID BERMAN

The Drinking Pig Company Ltd

McDonald's: "Vigorous beef makes you more vigorous"

PHOTO COURTESY ADRIA ROBLES-MORUA

Images of animals begging to be eaten disturb me. Our distance from the realities of the slaughterhouse keeps such food industry depictions of animals participating in – even celebrating – their own demise oddly palatable.

Even better: saveyourlogo.org

Distancing ourselves

PHOTO: DAVID BERMAN

Mohawk gasoline station sign,
Saskatoon, Saskatchewan

If you have been to Western Canada, you've likely seen signposts for the Mohawk gasoline station so often that it probably doesn't register with you as a caricature of an aboriginal. Would it be different if it proclaimed Jew Gasoline with a clever logo of an ultra-orthodox Jew in a tall black hat and curly sidelocks?

Mohawks are one of many proud First Nations in North America, and though I am certain no one meant any harm when they chose the Mohawk name for a chain of gas stations (any more than intended when sports franchise owners named the Atlanta Braves or the Washington Redskins), it should not be considered acceptable branding.

The transfer of pride from tribe to product in cars named Pontiac is so complete, few recall the origin of this brand. We often isolate what we admire in a group, without really understanding much about them. This unfortunately strengthens myths, while distancing us from the reality. The gap in health and living standards for Canada's aboriginal peoples compared to other Canadians has consistently widened over the past 50 years.[90] How do we remain so desensitized? Do these simple, shiny images help us push away a truer picture that is more messy to grapple with?

And if it is so with a minority, would you believe me if I told you we are doing a similar injustice to half our population?

"Possible ≠ desirable"

TERRY IRWIN

Global fantasy meets local reality on Hong Kong's Nathan Street, 2006

PHOTO: DAVID BERMAN

"You can tell the ideals of a nation by its advertisements."

NORMAN DOUGLAS (1868–1952)

6 WINE, WOMEN, AND WATER

THE MOST FAMILIAR APPROACH taken by designers who want to help sell more stuff is the misleading and manipulative coupling of sexy bodies with products.

Consider the ad below that ran full page in *Life* magazine more than 50 years ago.

This "playful" design shows what was considered acceptable in 1952 in the United States of America. Today, it seems unbelievable that one of the largest coffee brands would run this ad, and that the country's highest-circulating magazine of the day would print it. Some may be surprised at what the ad reveals regarding society's attitude towards women in the 1950s.

It is tempting to dismiss the ad as simply a reflection of the attitudes of the day. However, to what degree were such full page ads responsible for encouraging American men in 1952 that it was okay, even laudable, to beat their wives?

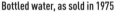

Bottled water, as sold in 1975   Bottled water, as sold in *Men's Health*, 2004

And what currently acceptable advertising running in our magazines today will an increasingly media-literate society look back upon as reprehensible 50 years from now? Ads continue to exploit women, though often with more subtlety.

A teenage mermaid seducing a bottle of water may convince America to burn its oil reserves to ship French water across the sea (to the continent with the world's largest fresh water supply). But does the means justify the end?

At the same time, what unreasonable expectations are we burying in the messages that we give our daughters today regarding the composition and use of their bodies?

Today's advertisers are clearly no longer as concerned with anti-sexist backlash as they were in the 1990s, a time when it

 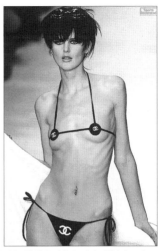

The first *Sports Illustrated* swimwear issue was published in 1964, legitimized the bikini, and changed the nature of modeling. Today, extreme women serve as billboards for fashion brands.

seemed that such imagery was fading from use in the West in keeping with the march of women's liberation. I am amongst those who thought this battle would soon be won, just as I thought we had successfully shifted away from subtly undermining the authority of women by referring to them as "girls."

As a genre of visual cliché becomes accepted in our society, the layering becomes increasingly subtle and derivative. It can be an enlightening exercise to systematically review the use of a particular device, through the spectrum of overt to subtle, delving into the layers.

Because using women's bodies is such a familiar technique, the next few pages demonstrate an abbreviated version of such an exploration.

DOING GOOD

I first met Amy Gendler, a designer from Omaha, Nebraska, at a design conference in Seattle. She was moving to China from Philadelphia to set up an AIGA office in Beijing. I visited her in 2006: there she was, supporting design education, exposing students in remote campuses to each other's work. The office has publications in Chinese, starting with their "Design Business and Ethics" series, thus helping to bring the next generation of China's designers into the world design economy in a more sustainable and ethical way. Amy teaches full-time at China's celebrated Central Academy of Fine Arts, thus helping to tackle everything from sans serif to social responsibility.

From the least subtle, where women's bodies are actually branded...

This bizarre combination of power imbalance, implied violence, and redefinition of "true love" results in the female model having her butt branded with the company logo.

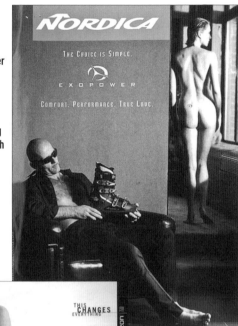

I can't see how Radeon would begin to defend that branding a woman's midriff has anything to do with video cards, however they could have at least reproduced their own logo correctly.

PHOTOS: DAVID BERMAN

These posters on the streets of Hong Kong are brand advertising for the women themselves .

...to the commonplace lazy marketing of using women's bodies to brazenly promote just about anything.

Brazil banned cartoon characters from selling drinks (hurrah!), but selling beer in grocery stores is still considered women's work.

Guess: where are the jeans?

Adding a warm, more human appeal to cold technology is tempting.

Sex sells computer magazines in Slovenia, as well as the United States

Ads like this sometimes make me truly embarrassed to be a designer.

Bus shelter, Budapest: So many phone features, so why focus on human features?

If all these pictures sell more books, are we guilty too?

Is it okay to use women to sell good ideas?

Sex helps sell a politician in the Czech Republic. Is this the best way to globalize democracy?

Or is this? On a related matter, is it okay to choose a candidate for her youth or sex appeal?

Is it okay to distort bodies in order to distort opinions?

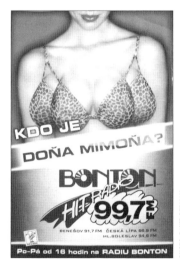

From out-of-control Photoshopping selling stereo radio in Prague...

...to subtly, impossibly lengthened legs selling toys in Tokyo

Often the context of who is speaking or where they are speaking is what makes the advertising inappropriate.

Of course it makes sense to show a woman in a bikini if bikinis are what you sell. But this ad appeared in *Men's Health* magazine. Men don't buy bikinis; it's a clever excuse to use women to sell the Nautica brand to men. (And what is going on in that shadow? Art directors don't let that stuff happen by accident.)

PHOTO: DAVID BERMAN

Body Shop ad, Vienna: the world's second-largest cosmetics company claims amongst its core values to "activate self-esteem."

This backlit advertisement, targeting youth, seems tame until you realize that the advertiser is Denmark's state-owned rail transportation system.

As society becomes more media-literate, a common ploy is to mock the styles of earlier decades. Now-forbidden stereotypes re-appear, as we are taken back to a time when they were status quo.

Do women really dress like this in Turkey? (And what do camels have to do with tobacco, anyhow?)

Mints by a tobacco company, curiously pitched with regressive charm by usually progressive *Utne Reader*

Not quite barefoot, silent, in the kitchen. The throwback theme doesn't justify the throwback humiliation.

Nor is it okay to recycle retired, deceptive branding for new markets, using questionably empowering slogans...

The Virginia Slims brand was famous in the 70s ("You've come a long way baby") for appropriating women's liberation to addict women to tobacco with a subtle promise of weight loss. Here the brand is resurrected to send an equally twisted "Find Your Voice" message to African women yet to discover throat cancer.

The solution is *not* to introduce false balance by exploiting men to an equal degree.

Is security really what is being sold here?

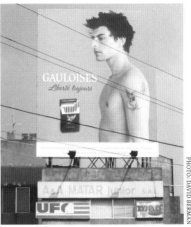

PHOTO: DAVID BERMAN

This Beirut billboard brands a man instead of a woman. The slogan translates to "freedom always," which couldn't be less true for a young nicotine addict.

The solution is to think, to be aware, to debate.

Then.
Pears' Soap ad from 1920s UK: a delightful parable of how Pears' soap is worth a chilly and precipitous climb from the tub, or simply the softest of kiddie porn?

Now.
Is this the most explicit image in this chapter? If you're willing to set aside the ethics of designer as pornography peddler, this promotion for Playboy's Dutch site launch is refreshingly creative. But then, perhaps lending sophistication to this industry is neither what men nor women need.

Dove's Campaign For Real Beauty certainly feels like part of the solution. It sells soap more truthfully, and yet goes beyond: positioning the brand as an overt agent of change. But these "real curves" ads were retouched as well. So is advertising masquerading as activism a deception of its own? Perhaps all activism is simply a form of advertising?

The solution is to respect everyone. The solution is to use the power we have responsibly and sensitively. The solution is to imagine a society where the loudest, largest messages are those that not only promote healthy behaviors but also embrace metaphors that reinforce them as well.

Here's a delightful, on-message, respectful ad where people are nude ...yet not naked.

DOING GOOD When I met Lise Klint in 2003 at a sustainable design class in Denmark, she was still in the private sector, while President of the Danish national design association. We excitedly shared our beliefs that better governance and ISO compliance can transform design organizations globally. Lise is now director of INDEX, a non-profit based in her country. INDEX's global network of designers, businesses, organizations, and institutions collaborate in applying cutting-edge knowledge to the challenge of "Design to Improve Life." Funded by the State of Denmark, INDEX offers the largest design award in the world.: "I truly believe that if you have the ability to respond to problems then you also have the responsibility to do so. We call that respondability. And it makes you happy to go to work each morning."

McMemories
The Official McDonald's Collectibles Club™

What a Treat — His First McDonald's French Fries!

Approximately 12" head to toe (9" seated as shown). Poseable. With McDonald's french fries and costuming shown. Hand-numbered Certificate of Authenticity included. Issued in a strictly hand-numbered edition.

- Three installments of $21.80*
- Certificate of Authenticity
- 365-day guarantee
- Authorized by McDonald's

McMemories 9305 Milwaukee Ave. Niles IL 60714

With a smile on his face and a sparkle in his baby blue eyes, "Eric" is having the time of his life. He's enjoying his very first order of delicious french fries with Mom and Dad at McDonald's. What fun it is to nibble them one at a time, to make them last! "Eric" is the first issue in the *Treats for Tots* doll collection by world-renowned doll artist Yolanda Bello, featuring happy babies enjoying McDonald's treats for the first time. He's a superbly crafted fine-porcelain collectible doll from McMemories — the Official McDonald's Collectibles Club. He comes with cotton-blend romper and sunhat — and an order of "french fries."

Re-live a child's joy with "Eric." Outstanding value at only $59.95. *Fully guaranteed.* Order today.

©1997 McDonald's Corporation
McDonald's, McMemories, Golden Arches, and Golden Arches logo are trademarks of McDonald's Corporation   95888-CC3A

McMemories
The Official McDonald's Collectibles Club™
9305 N. Milwaukee Avenue, Niles, IL 60714-1380

PLEASE RESPOND BY: MAY 31, 1997
YES. Please enter my reservation for "Eric's First French Fries." I need SEND NO MONEY NOW. I will be billed in three monthly installments of just $21.80* each (includes $5.44 postage and handling), the first payable before shipment. Item not available in restaurants.

Name _____
(Please print clearly)
Address _____
City _____
State _____ Zip _____
Phone(_____) _____

*Illinois residents please add state sales tax. Please allow 6 to 8 weeks for delivery. The prices of the products and the shipping fees are higher in Canada.   30371-D86101

In 2007, McDonald's agreed to cease marketing to kids under 12.

"Design awakens all the senses"
LEE KUN-HEE, SAMSUNG

7 LOSING OUR SENSES

A PRODUCT'S DESIGN CAN BECOME more strategically important than the product itself. Branded products double as advertising for the brand. So as brands evolve from marks of quality to free-floating ideas, products also become intentional vectors of brand awareness.

Considering the lengths that breweries will go to influence males aged 18 to 24, it is clear that those companies have figured out the transcendence of branding. Marketers and designers know that the beer men buy while young will likely be the beer they'll reach for throughout their lives.

It's a rare person who can distinguish mainstream lagers without their labels. Rather, brewers exploit the fact that people use a particular beer brand to make a statement about themselves. Which bottle they choose to display at their pub table advertises something about who they are.[91]

PHOTO: DAVID BERMAN

False beer cases with false hopes, corner store, Montréal

SOLUT PERFECTION.

ABSOLUT GREED.

ABSOLUT IMPOTENCE.

COURTESY ADBUSTERS

"Which of these ads is not like the other?" It's hard to tell the real Absolut ads from the spoof.

Companies tend to brand most intensely those products that are most difficult to tell apart, such as bottled water, alcohol – even politicians. When there is no substantive difference, marketers manufacture a distinction. Absolut vodka is famous for seizing the U.S. vodka market with a delightful advertising campaign, outselling bourbon in its home market. In chemical analysis, all non-traditional clear vodkas are essentially identical – as my dad demonstrated in his National Research Council lab, where he spent his entire career. Knowing that competitors would not be able to produce a higher-quality liquid, Absolut instead created this famously clever campaign, where the product becomes whatever a specific target audience takes pride in.

Corporations and marketing campaigns are changing the way we all think about our world. As I travel, I find myself explaining to people who have never spent time in North America that it is not the place depicted in advertisements or soap operas or Hollywood films. North America is not Coca-Cola, Marlboro, and KFC. We are different, diverse, greater than the sum of all products, worthy of pride. We are proud of our governance, our heritage, our history. We are proud of our innovation. But there is a lot we should not be so proud of...

Teaching kids to smoke and eat junk: how logo can we go?

Before the Joe Camel cartoon character appeared in the 1980s, Camel cigarettes had one percent of the U.S. teen cigarette market. By the

time Joe was deported in 1997, Camel had 32 percent of this market,[92] and more than 90 percent of six-year-olds could recognize Joe (more than knew Mickey Mouse).[93] Is there any question that these ads were targeting youth?

The ad below contains no branding, no product shot, no benefit statement. Yet Marlboro branding is so prevalent that, typographer or not, you just need to see the font[94] to recognize the brand. Philip Morris International rolls out more than 760 billion cigarettes a year.[95] That's almost six packs for every man, grandmother, and child on the planet.

The world's longest-running advertising campaign,[96] born in 1954, sadly will outlive most smokers.

So will Big Tobacco succeed in convincing the girl using the sip-puff technology to puff cigarettes?

DOING GOOD In 1989, veteran advertising executive Trevor Field happened upon a children's merry-go-round attached to a water pump at an agricultural fair outside of Johannesburg. By 1994, Trevor had redesigned it, adding a high-capacity water tank and four billboard spaces for public education messages. Today, more than 1,000 PlayPumps have been donated to schools and communities in South Africa. Now over 10 million people have clean drinking water, pumped by children at play in 10 countries in Eastern and Southern Africa.

Lying to children is especially heinous.[97] Methodically tricking a population that still believes in the tooth fairy in order to fulfill a greed disorder lies somewhere between cowardly and despicable. And yet, U.S. advertisers spend more than $12 billion a year on messages aimed at the youth market.[98]

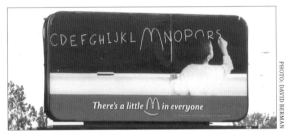

PHOTO: DAVID BERMAN

"Over 100 billion sold." [99]
The M logo was designed by Jim Schindler in 1962.

McDonald's set out many years ago to make their letter M part of every child's alphabet, with a specific focus on long-term marketing targeted at young children. A generation later, the average weight of an American has risen over 4.5 kg (10 pounds). Consider that Americans spend 42 percent of their food budget on food served outside the home, compared to 27 percent in Canada. One-fifth of the mass of municipal solid waste in the U.S. today is food packaging,[100] while obesity kills 325,000 Americans a year – more than alcohol, drugs, firearms, and motor vehicles combined.[101]

McDonald's marketing at naïve five-year-olds was predatory. A typical American child sees 10,000 food commercials a year on television,[102] sprinkled among increasingly violent TV shows designed to build brand identity: almost every cartoon show is about a product line. American children have more pocket money than the world's half-billion poorest people,[103] and one in three American kids under six has a TV in his or her room.

"Contempt for the intelligence of the audience engenders graphics that lie... graphic excellence begins with telling the truth." EDWARD R. TUFTE

To convince children of a world full of false needs is downright cruel. Would you invite someone into your home that would lie to your kids? Of course not. So why would we invite people into our workplaces who want us to help them trick children?

Consider that of the 111 songs that made the Billboard Top 20 of 2003 – a list biased heavily towards youth-driven pop culture – 43 had brand names within the lyrics.[104]

The age at which children recognize that advertising is not always truthful is around eight.[105] At what age will a child stop putting their tooth under the pillow for the tooth fairy? Even in the face of contradictory evidence, children will hold onto beliefs about Santa Claus for years. And there are many subtler deceptions that stick with us our entire lives.

In North America, our 10-year-olds have learned to some degree how the lying works. They build up a certain immunity, a skeptical thick skin, and prematurely lose some childhood sensitivity. The larger risks lie in larger populations rapidly embracing the worst of Western lifestyle, not only proliferating overconsumption, waste, and foreign dependence, but also undermining culture that would provide stability through times of great change.

PHOTO: DAVID BERMAN

Sexualization and celebrity are changing what childhood is about

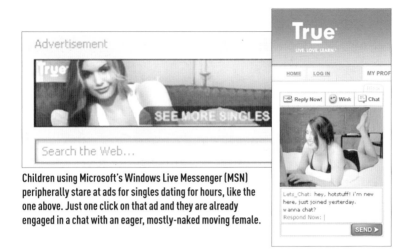

Children using Microsoft's Windows Live Messenger (MSN) peripherally stare at ads for singles dating for hours, like the one above. Just one click on that ad and they are already engaged in a chat with an eager, mostly-naked moving female.

Bombarding young audiences with persuasive messages is additionally unethical because teenagers are so easily influenced as they desperately seek and shape their identities. Young people today are wonderfully savvy of the tactics being used against them, and yet they still remain victims.

We can do better: in the Canadian province of Québec, and the countries of Sweden and Norway, television advertising aimed at children is prohibited by law.[106]

By the time students reach high school, they have already been socialized to expect a bombardment of marketing messaging. I recently visited my old high school and found there are now national pizza chain ads in the lunch area. In a vacuum of funding for the poorer U.S. schools, 8,000 principals happily agreed to force children to watch advertising-based Channel One News in the

COURTESY ADBUSTERS

Time to reflect

classroom, in exchange for free television equipment. At their desks, this programming teaches kids to consume fast food, candy bars, and sports drinks. Meanwhile, in the U.S., 13 percent of schools allow fast-food chains to operate on their premises.[107]

And then our kids become college students. If the ethical argument is not compelling enough, consider the geopolitical effects of exporting confusion, inferiority, and desensitization to the parts of the world where extremist groups also offer identity education to vulnerable youths with low self-esteem. In October 2002, I was travelling in a bus to an ethics seminar for design students in Jordan about the effects of bombardment by foreign icons of success, beauty, and power. I casually counted that the people in four out of five billboards in Amman were obviously Western. These images defining success, attractiveness, and what you need to be loved and admired, are what these youth are encouraged to emulate.

The students reported a prevailing feeling of inferiority. One student put it this way: "We know we are behind and not as good as those people." And I wonder to what degree this belief was learned from a lifetime barrage of oppressive imagery.

PHOTO: DAVID BERMAN

Unsatisfied Europeans and English in Byblos, Lebanon

Such marketing plays on the relative naïveté of Developing World cultures as much as it plays on the higher vulnerability of a child who has not grown up in a culture of visual deceit. The Jordanian youth are, admirably, not socialized to be victims of visual lies.

Our inner child

Ania, a designer who had immigrated to Canada from pre-democratic Poland, came to work at my design studio. One day she received a Publishers Clearing House sweepstakes letter at her home, explaining in colorful detail how she apparently had just won over $1 million. She was understandably bouncing off the walls in excitement until her Canadian partner arrived home to give her the sobering, humiliating news that no, that's just a very fancy deception that we are all accustomed to here in North America.

There are so many lies like these within our socialization that we don't even notice anymore. How much does that thickened skin cost our society? **And what are we getting in return?**

Macau is being transformed into an offshore gambling haven for over a billion Chinese in whose country gambling is against the law. I've never seen so many cranes in one place.

As adults, we find it often impossible to break habits, especially those learned early on. Advertisers take advantage of weaknesses in our psyche to convince us of false needs that can be satisfied by buying things. Good design should be about what's good about the product, not what is "bad" or vulnerable in the buyer.

The slot machine is an ingenious piece of industrial design that assists in the triumph of the greedy over the vulnerable. The device hugely magnifies a combination of subtle weaknesses in the human decision-making schema – a schema which works excellently for mammals in the natural wild, but is dangerously burdensome in an artificial urban world. The effect is amplified by an eerily satisfying mixture of feedback many cannot ignore. The resulting methodical corruption of judgment often destroys the hopes and dreams of individuals and their families, creating poverty and crime. Even more troubling, our acceptance addicts governments to a carcinogen of unnatural profit. And so, rather than regulating safer entertainment, govern-ment enjoys reaping regressive gambling taxes, spending just enough on a public display of brochures and hotlines to suggest that the situation is under control.

PHOTO: DAVID BERMAN

Tokyo: Is this how we want our children spending their days and their earnings? Fulfilling primeval urges to hunt and gather through habituated shopping can be just as intense.

Shopping is more subtle than gambling, but no matter how logical I believe my buying decisions to be, beloved radio jingles are still in my head from when I was five years old.

Similarly, the seed for the success of the subprime mortgage sales pitch was planted decades ago. As children, we were taught by our own society that bankers teach us how to save, and to rely upon our friendly banker to be more cautious with our money than our own risk impulses would typically dictate.

Common sense of smell

Does giving up our sense of smell make us lose our sense of right and wrong?

We have become so accustomed to the association of perfume and sex in advertising that it no longer registers as unnatural. My tweenage nephews are now wearing Axe cologne. I'm not sure if they know why. They are being trained that wearing (or perhaps just purchasing) false pheromones will yield passionate intimacy and Hollywood hair. In the West, perfumes and sexual imagery are so linked that the very notion of how we are supposed to experience emotional and physical intimacy are defined for us by advertisers.

"And when did the fine art of perfumery go from being about taboo, love potions and sorcery to Bill Blass, Christian Dior and Ralph Lauren?"

TOM ROBBINS, IN *JITTERBUG PERFUME*

What would Maslow do?

Calvin Klein pioneered online personas, giving these fictions e-mail addresses

I wonder if those young men will ever be able to experience sexuality without the overlays taught by print, television and the Internet. (It would be as difficult as seeing Harry Potter as you had imagined him while reading, before you'd seen the movie of the book.)

Must their first kiss be a Kodak Moment? Can we not own our own intimacy? I do not want to think about Calvin Klein when I am making love – do you? The natural, evolutionary link between our sense of smell and mating behaviors has become horribly contorted by the forces of greed. The social profit-and-loss statement on this transaction is unlikely to be in society's favor.

What drives all this energy and motivation to create ever-larger mechanisms to convince our most vulnerable to choose behaviors clearly not in their best interests, nor in the best interests of our species?

You can have a balanced life. But cologne won't give it to you. Disney's Mickey Eisner coined the term "branded experience," as something to be sought out.

white picket fence

DOING GOOD It's difficult to keep up with Eric Benson. He was working as a print designer in Ann Arbor in 2000 when "I saw how much of my work was ending up in the trash. It was beautiful, but was it responsible?" Inspired by books like *Cradle To Cradle* he chose to study sustainable design in grad school. His life is now about environmentally responsible design: his re-nourish.com site is a favorite of many designers. I met Eric working together on developing a system for global sustainable design practices. "The world is changing, and we can be at the forefront."

"gre

is a bottomless pit."
CONOR OBERST

Greed for resources. Greed for power. More resources and power than any one person or family could ever really make use of. It's simply an unfortunate aberration: the drive behind such greed is a healthy instinct shared by all mammals, coupled with a healthy pushback from a natural environment that is uncompromising in its power. But evolution was not prepared for a species to come along and blow past the assumed limits: a species that figured out how to rearrange the resources so that this drive could be so grandly and regularly overfulfilled. The unfortunate result: a society caught up in seeking more rather than enjoying what we have; a society that often celebrates success by what we can acquire rather than what we do.

Advertising and design change how youth behave and think. Do you really want to spend the best years of your career spreading misery and feelings of inadequacy? Encouraging addictions? Destroying hopes and dreams? Perhaps it is professionals who should be changing their thinking instead.

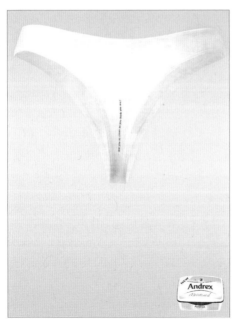

"Are you as clean as you think you are?"
Typographic excellence boldly questioning self-esteem.

Let's not just help turn the ship around while there is still time. Let's ask ourselves who is at the helm, and why we let them lead. Is our ship being steered by a great philosophical vision, or has it simply been hijacked by a natural mammalian tendency, artificially magnified beyond reason or value?

Those who lead always have ulterior motives.

Conspicuous powers

Does enough integrity exist among professionals and consumers that we can volunteer to help navigate the ship?

Society wisely confers conspicuous power and stewardship to professional groups. **Design has a disproportionately large influence in these three areas:**

1. **How messages intended to influence the behavior of large audiences are selected, crafted, and delivered**
2. **How people are portrayed and represented visually**
3. **How raw materials for designed objects (such as the paper for this book) are consumed**

The Many Faces of David Berman typeface catalogue, David Berman Typographics, 1989

Are designers behaving in a way that encourages society to fully entrust them with such stewardship?

Once upon a time, all I cared about what has how good the typography was. One day I realized that, no matter how well I perfect the spacing of a headline, if the words won't fulfill the client's strategy, my effort is pointless. But the larger news hit me later: if that message is counterproductive to the larger strategy of a sustainable world, then my effort is also irresponsible.

I hope that I've made this message clear: the biggest issue of our day is the environment; overconsumption is driving its destruction; overconsumption is fueled most powerfully by clever visual arguments to convince everyone (including larger, growing Developing World populations) to consume more and more. The impact of designers and consumers of design is huge. We should be held responsible.

Why must we take responsibility?

Because we can.

"With great power comes great responsibility"

SPIDER-MAN'S UNCLE BEN

"Class A" kitten, Zanzibar market

FILTER CIGARETTES

Marlboro

20 CLASS A CIGARETTES

PHOTO: DAVID BERMAN

the design
convenient truths

LEO BURNETT SOUTH AFRICA

JACQUELINE GERMIN

Salvation Army poster doubles as a blanket a homeless person can pull off the wall to use

Designer clothes made entirely from pop cans, newsprint, and other "garbage"

solution:

DAVID BERMAN/CHRISTIAN JENSEN

Humor encouraging diversity at work:
design where everyone belongs

The church fights to reclaim Christmas:
What would Jesus design?

The actor who actually portrayed the Marlboro Man died of cancer at the age of 51.

COURTESY CALIFORNIA DEPARTMENT OF HEALTH SERVICES

WARNING: SMOKING CAUSES IMPOTENCE

> "We can't solve problems by using the same kind of thinking we used when we created them."
>
> ALBERT EINSTEIN (1879–1955)

8 WHY OUR TIME IS THE PERFECT TIME

IF YOU'RE STILL READING, you're likely already convinced that there are numerous ethical arguments for change. Now let's explore why the timing has never been better – or more profitable – for responsible design.

What's your favorite typeface? *Century Oldstyle (BUT DON'T TELL ERIK)*

When I started my design firm over 20 years ago, if you hadn't gone to art school or seen the inside of a type shop, it's unlikely you'd know what a font was. When I was a kid we had favorite colors. Today, not only do both my daughter and her friends have favorite typefaces, but my mother also knows what small caps and kerning are!

Just 15 years ago, it was unheard of to see cover stories in *BusinessWeek, Time,* and *Report on Business* on design, branding and identity. With design successes like the iPad and iPhone revitalizing Apple to the point of now being worth more than Microsoft and IBM, big business is realizing that design is, as former Kodak CEO George Fisher puts it, an integral part of business strategy.[108]

Brand equity is showing up on the balance sheets of an increasing number of corporations. Designers and what they do have never been as valued as they are today, and that gives us the opportunity (as well as the duty) to responsibly use design to make a difference.

Ethical design is also profitable design: both client and designer make more money in the long term by making a promise to customers that is later fulfilled. Sell me a car by implying that it will get me more sex, by draping half-naked models over the hood in advertising photos, and you *may* increase your chance of selling one car. Ultimately, however, the reality will fall short of the promise, and next time I'll shop for a different brand.

PHOTO: DAVID BERMAN

In 1998, Pantone® color chips were only known to designers. In 2008, they had become the branded theme of designer cell phones in this Japanese store.

Sell me a Mercury coupe based upon the fable of the car as a toy that I can drive on mythical open roads where I won't see another vehicle for hours, and I will certainly be disappointed.

New Mercury Cougar. Imagine yourself in a Mercury
front-wheel drive •optional V # •hatchback •800-446-8888 •www.mercuryvehicles.com

Granted, you could sell someone a car for its status symbol value alone. However, cars are tools, not toys. More Americans have died in car crashes in the last 100 years than in all the foreign wars the U.S. has ever fought.[109]

Ethical design and promotion can be the most efficient marketing. Getting excellent products into the hands of consumers with tangible needs, through clear communication that delights and informs, is a profitable, sustainable business. Meanwhile, misleading promotion can injure brands (and people) by creating waste and disappointment.

History demonstrates this truth on a massive scale. Starting in the 1970s, while U.S. car manufacturers were busy pitching autos based upon trite annual fashion changes, the Japanese were busy designing better cars. They replaced Henry Ford's legendary production line philosophy of driving down costs with the continuous improvement philosophy of the American W. Edwards Deming,

which stresses improving quality by producing small quantities, testing, then tweaking the design. Within 15 years, the Japanese industry had shifted gears, from producing cars that Americans laughed at to ones Americans preferred. The result: today, Toyota and Honda share the four top positions on the U.S. best-selling car chart.[110] More telling is that Americans vote for their higher appreciation of design with their wallets, forking over an additional $3,000 or more for that higher quality.[111] In other words, Americans have internalized the value of better design. Over the next few years, they will pay a premium again, to have their next car be a hybrid (again led by the Japanese) or electric, which is good business for our fragile planet.

Any auto industry marketing maven would agree that the greatest profit is to be made not by selling you one new car, but by selling you many cars throughout your lifetime. And so rather than convince you to buy one Toyota, they are wise to teach you how to recognize the quality that the Toyota brand consistently represents. If you learn that Toyotas tend to fit your needs, you learn to trust the Toyota brand. In order for this to work, you do need a product that has reliably excellent properties, and is appropriate for a given buyer. Consider two ways of selling an excellent car:

APPROACH #1: "Now here's a car for you: clever features, great fuel efficiency, high safety rating. See how much care we've put into the design, feel how comfortable and delightful it is to operate, imagine how safe your family will be. If this is what you're looking for in a car, now and for a long time to come, you should buy our Canyonero because we offer what you need at a price that is sensible for you." If I buy that car I'll very likely be satisfied, not just for a month, but for many years; I will become fiercely loyal and perhaps buy a new Canyonero every decade for the rest of my life.

"You know you're not the first": this used car ad earns the checkered flag for how many ways it offends

APPROACH #2: "Buy this car and you'll become really rich. Buy this car and people will think you are smarter than you really are. Buy this car and you'll have lots more sex." We know how the human brain is hardwired: by showing me a picture of a car with a sexy celebrity I enjoy, or showing the car doing fun things that cars aren't really intended to do, you can successfully play on my desire to imagine a future where I am more than I am. You are trying to sell me a fantasy, not a car. And you may well trick me into buying something that isn't right for me. You may even have an excellent product, but it's now in the hands of the wrong person. Will I buy another Canyonero in 10 years? Probably not. Because at some level, I will feel dissatisfied; maybe even realize I've been lied to, ripped off. And the next time – no matter

Selling good features can be fun too

how well your next model would fit my needs – I'll look elsewhere, fueled by both reason and resentment.

However, if you'd been straight with me, then either then, now, or at some future appropriate time, you could have fulfilled lasting needs and have earned my lasting brand loyalty. And chances are that I'd tell my friends about that too.

Smoke and mirrors

So, we can design a better car, and we can promote its merits to the appropriate buyer. However, with a product like the cigarette, that has little to no merit – no foreign country is going to come up with a "better" cigarette. Rather, the competition for cigarettes (and for other products that simply hurt us) is a well-educated public. This is exactly what design has the power to help create. We have the power to communicate accurate, clear, useful messages that reach and inform millions.

The more educated a society becomes, the more Big Tobacco scrambles to light up markets that are either less educated about the hazards of their product or less protected from their predatory communication strategies. Hence the huge marketing focus on the Developing World, where ad campaigns relentlessly push tactics no longer tolerated in the West.

Imagine again a society's potential where the largest signs, the cleverest ads, the most prominent messages promote healthy behaviors. Isn't that the society we want our children to grow up in? We can choose it now.

Jacques Lange is creative director at Bluprint Design, a South African firm with clients who contribute to quality of life. "The role of design is to use technology, systems, information, spaces and environments to improve the human condition, no matter the current condition." My favorite project of his was with the SABS Design Institute. In April 2005, Bluprint promoted and managed an "Interdesign" on sustainable rural transport near Rustenburg. For two weeks, 70 local and international designers worked with villagers to find transportation solutions for the harsh local conditions, focusing on animal-drawn carts, alternative modes of transport, and communication. The result: 19 strong concepts. Prototypes and instructions were donated to the community to spawn small business growth.

DOING GOOD

~~Don't~~ Shoot The Messenger

In July 2000, a Florida jury told the tobacco industry to pay an award of $145 billion, the largest punitive damages award ever handed down anywhere. The previous world record was a $5 billion fine against ExxonMobil for the *Exxon Valdez* oil spill that devastated the Pacific ecosystem off the Alaska coast in 1989.

Neither settlement lasted intact upon appeal.[112] Nonetheless, if you had wandered into the smoke-filled Virginia boardrooms of Big Tobacco 25 years ago, suggesting that someone start worrying about such future penalties, you would have been laughed out of the state.

What degree of responsibility do designers have for the offenses that led to that court decision in Florida? Aren't the ad and package designers just as guilty of promoting destructive behaviors? They had access to the strategies that laid out the mechanisms of nicotine addiction and tricking people into trying to smoke.

Coca-Cola red fills in for Big Tobacco brown

So how long until the agencies, the art directors, and the designers get sued along with their tobacco company clients? Designers who dream up visual lies cannot hide behind the communications strategy documents aimed at shortening children's lives for profit, claiming they "were just following orders." It wasn't an acceptable excuse for Eichmann, nor for Milošević's men, and it's not acceptable for designers either.

Social responsibility is also good for design because it will protect the profession. Consider what happened to the accounting profession in the late 1990s or the financial industry in 2008: they allowed their professional conduct to slip below society's level of what's acceptable, and the damage to both continues to resonate. A profession that fails to offer ethical solutions will correctly be accused of telling lies in order to succeed. Hey, designers, were you lying then or are you lying now?

Design for the people, by the people

Much of my proudest work has been for Canada's Tobacco Control Programme, and when speaking outside my country, I've shocked many audiences with samples of the graphics adorning Canadian cigarette packaging since 2000.

In Canada, our tobacco industry is mandated to display pictures of diseased lungs, graphs of mortality rates, and other vivid demonstrations of what the consumer is lighting into, on every pack. This packaging law, combined with Canada's strict limitations on tobacco advertising, is one of the world's most impressive examples of a society saying enough is enough! The common sense

PHOTOS: DAVID BERMAN

Canada's pioneering visual warnings required by law, including instructions on how to quit inside every pack, have been featured in Manhattan's Museum of Modern Art.

underlying Canada's controls on tobacco marketing has been borne out by public health studies demonstrating a correlating drop in smoking six years after the packaging laws came into force.[113]

Considered preposterous a decade earlier, the Canadian model that put strong, graphic antismoking warnings right in our faces has been adopted by countries

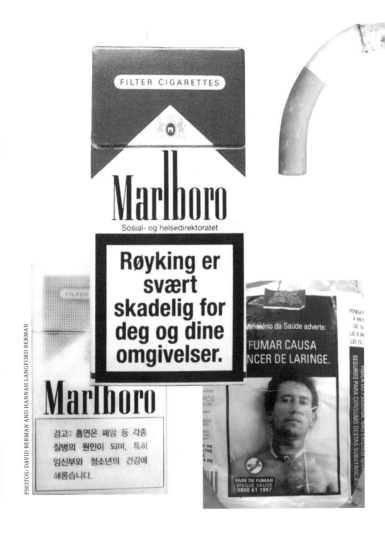

PHOTOS: DAVID BERMAN AND HANNAH LANGFORD BERMAN

DOING GOOD I first worked with Nova Scotia designer Brenda Sanderson on the GDC executive. In 2005 she put a healthy career in the ad world on indefinite hold to take a job as managing director of Icograda, the world body for communication design, setting up their new headquarters in Montréal (now also headquarters for the world bodies for industrial and interior design, forming one International Design Alliance). Icograda seeks "to advance the best interests of humanity and the ecology, through design." We're working together developing greener event and global sustainable design best practices. I firmly believe that the 'small group of committed citizens' that sparked Margaret Mead's imagination were designers. This group is growing, both in numbers and in its commitment to progressive change."

around the world. And similar type or graphics now appear on cigarette packages throughout the EU, Brazil, and Australia. Meanwhile, in New York City, tobacco advertising, by law, must be at least 100 yards (90 meters) from schools.

In 2008, the display of cigarettes in stores was banned in entire cities and regions in Canada and Australia. Why? Because the arrays of cigarette packages were effectively point-of-purchase displays for smoking, to be restricted like any other advertisement.

Of course, clever tobacco marketers will keep trying to burn holes in legislation. In Europe, when Camel cigarette billboard ads were banned, Camel brand matches appeared. Armed with their keen understanding of how branding matters more than actual

PHOTO: HANNAH LANGFORD BERMAN

Donna's Express covers up its cigarettes, in compliance with Ontario law

PHOTO: DAVID BERMAN

Chocolate cigarettes for sale to children, in a Montréal store that can no longer display real cigarettes

product, in the 1990s
tobacco shillers dreamed up
Camel concerts, Camel
watches, Camel lighters,
Camel comic books, Camel

PHOTO: DAVID BERMAN

matches, and Camel travel expeditions. In Germany, Camel boots
actually peaked at 7.5 percent of the market share for all men's
shoe sales![114] By 2001, the EU banned all non-point-of-sale tobacco
advertising, including "brand stretching" (such as sponsoring
sporting and cultural events). The bizarre spinoff: teams of tobacco
industry lawyers hired to prove their clients' incompetence as
businesspeople, desperately trying to prove that the advertising
investment has no effect on tobacco sales.

Tobacco sponsorship like this is now banned in Canada

Son of Marlboro Man?

Dar Es Salaam, Tanzania: the local Marlboro lookalike contrasts with an unexpected protest poster

Meanwhile, in lands that lack limits on advertising, the battle for the lungs of our daughters and sons rages on.

The Indian Tobacco Company (ITC), India's leading cigarette maker, is working with the government. Recognizing that continuing to promote smoking to a billion people is not in the national interest, yet not wanting to dismantle an industry, the plan is to perform a healthier version of brand stretching. Rather than apply the cigarette brand to other products as a way of sneakily promoting cigarettes, ITC is earnestly investigating how to apply the successful brand to other products. They would leave the cigarette business behind while retaining the equity value of the brand. ITC is shifting India's most valuable cigarette brand, Wills Navy Cut, entirely to non-tobacco products. It is also seeking to redeploy its production and packaging plants to transform the leading Gold Flake brand to greeting cards, and its supply chain into 2,000 greeting card outlets. The company can thus use its brand equity and packaging expertise to celebrate birthdays, rather than eliminate them.

Freedom of speech

Are we unfairly limiting freedom of speech when we limit visual messages that convince people to damage themselves and others? Are we unfairly limiting tobacco companies' right to earn a buck? Legislating controls on the advertising of addictive products such

PHOTO: DAVID BERMAN

Smoke-free airport, Frankfurt

as tobacco is as reasonable as choosing to protect society by legislating speed limits, seat belts, and daytime running lights on our roads.

The epic battle against Big Tobacco is being won, city by city, country by country. You cannot even smoke in the street in Tokyo's Akihabara electronics district. Over 140 colleges in the United States have banned smoking outright. And as with Ralph Nader's victories with car safety in the 1960s, we won't be going back. Meanwhile, the model of scrutiny the tobacco industry has been brought under is being extended to other threats, such as child obesity, with the intelligent and caring mixture of individual, industry, and government action required to solve such issues.

PHOTO: THOMAS RYMER

The battle rages above our streets: Russia banned hard liquor billboard and TV spots in 2002, so "Stolichnaya story" is a photo contest, but Muscovites know they're selling vodka. Thomas Rymer explains: "If you can't understand what a commercial is about, that means it's vodka."

Safer cigarettes

And it turns out that we *can* design a better cigarette after all: in Canada, aside from providing a slow legal method of suicide, cigarettes also cause 4,000 house fires and over $50 million in property damage a year.[115] Or they did until Canada became the first country in the world to insist upon "fire-safe" cigarettes. It took over 70 years for the cigarette companies to agree (and why did we need their agreement?) to a 1932 self-extinguishing cigarette design that burns slower (and thus at a cooler, safer temperature). Fire-safe cigarettes have been the law in New York state since 2004, and 37 other U.S. states have since followed suit.[116]

Blind justice

Perhaps the greatest reason for hope is the evidence of rising visual literacy. Across the world, you can get sued for lying with words. However we are increasingly evolving into a visually literate society. As much as graphic designers often wince when they see how desktop publishing and the Internet have enabled almost everyone to

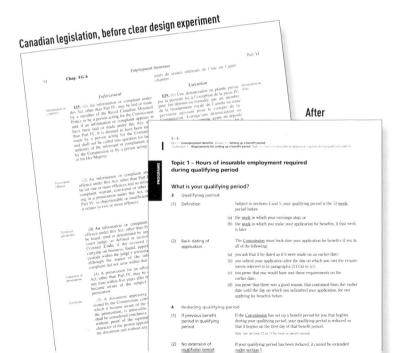

Canadian legislation, before clear design experiment

After

publish documents that painfully contain too many typefaces, that same immersion is creating a society with the nascent vocabulary to define and legislate against lying with pictures.

Making law more accessible is a communications challenge that can enhance the quality of a democracy: imagine a land where everyone has equal access to the law. In working with Canada's Department of Justice on a project to rewrite and redesign the laws of Canada in clear language and clear design, we envisioned legislation that everyone can access on paper or online – and understand without a lawyer's help. While working on this, we found a remarkable example of the truth in Edward Tufte's[117] assertion that to visualize information is to reveal new information. We decided to try including a flow chart within the Employment Insurance legislation to help explain and index the law. The process of developing the flowchart caused us to uncover a branch in the logic that the lawmakers had neglected to cover! The discovery was a puzzle, as a tenet of the project was that the meaning of the law could not be altered by the application of clear language and clear design.

Perfect storm

A perfect storm of increasing visual literacy, rising awareness, and collaborative technology makes this a perfect time to embrace design as a solution. And though MIT's Nicholas Negroponte, chair of One Laptop Per Child, reminds us that for over four billion humans the Internet remains a rumor,[118] change is on the move, and hope has never been more actionable... or more likely.

DOING GOOD It seems that every time I come to a country that is new to me, designers ask about Robert L. Peters. Sometimes "Robert Peters" is the only phrase we have in common, and excitedly so, as if we are in some action hero B-movie. In the mid-80s, Rob was inspired by people like Walter Jungkind, FGDC, who opened Rob's eyes to the international world of design. Rob and I became friends in a Montréal Lambada bar on Ste-Catherine Street in 1991, and I haven't seen him stop since. To summarize his influence internationally would fill the page with acronyms; however, it's the network, what Rob calls the "cross-pollination," that is his greatest legacy: a catalyst for the synergistic opportunities born when isolated designers in far-off parts of the world connect.

Monstrous shopping cart pushing popular brands for Spinneys supermarket, highway to Beirut

PHOTO: DAVID BERMAN

"I have not observed men's honesty to increase with their riches." THOMAS JEFFERSON (1743–1826)

9 HOW TO LIE, HOW TO TELL THE TRUTH

OUR SOCIETY HAS A LEGAL CODE that is based on words. We're trained to recognize word-based lies. The most subtle of inaccurate innuendo in words uttered by a politician can resonate for many news cycles ... or even end a career.

But because of our relatively low visual literacy, it's not as obvious to us when images have been cleverly strung together to create a visual lie. When a sentence is made up of pictures, and the sentence is not truthful, we're less likely to call a foul. Lies in words are controlled with libel and fraud laws, while subtle visual lies are often not – and so many creative liars can continue to operate with impunity.

A well-crafted visual lie can easily outperform a lie built solely of words. This is because images provoke subconscious, visceral reactions. The imagery can be so subtle that people often don't realize they are being manipulated.

PHOTO: DAVID BERMAN

Red cross brand on pharmacy in Macau

Humans excel at real-time pattern recognition: your brain constantly edits visual input, even before you are conscious of it. Your built-in Steadicam is constantly editing what comes in, without you being aware of the process. To demonstrate this to yourself, hold a smartphone on your shoulder, press Record, walk twenty steps, then compare the smooth image you perceived to the jerky, bouncy recorded image that actually met your eyes. This is why reading when the bus is on a rough road can be nauseating: the mental Steadicam gets overloaded and demands to be shut off. We are completely unaware of the extensive adjustment to raw sensory data going on upon arrival into our brains.

The annual productivity loss due to people having to process spam e-mails is measured in billions of dollars. And we all actively hate spam because we are conscious of spam: it is not only an annoyance to have to wade through, it also interrupts our focus on important things. However, what do you suppose is the annual loss due to the spamming of our unconscious with advertising, where the overload presents itself in the form of low-level stress, unexplained shopping, and skewed behavior, rather than nausea?

Two hundred years ago a person could go days without an ad interrupting your thoughts. The only time I go more than a night without seeing ads is if I'm in a hospital bed or on a canoe trip.

Forests, filters, and FedEx

To survive in the forest, we also evolved the skill of processing an overwhelming amount of information, gleaning what matters based on what we are already know. Try this: read the following sentence out loud **only once**, and as you go, count how many times you see the letter *F*. Ready? Go.

FEDEX FORMS ARE THE RESULT OF MANY YEARS OF CUSTOMER FEEDBACK COMBINED WITH THE EXPERIENCE OF MANY DESIGNERS.

How many *F*s did you count?

If you noticed all six, the chances are that English isn't your mother tongue. You were even more likely to find them all if you did not grow up with the Roman alphabet. If you show this to a child, they would probably score higher than you did.

If we can miss what is really going in such a straightforward situation as reading a sentence, imagine how much else we miss every hour because of our cultural and experiential filters. Now imagine how easily someone could manipulate us, taking advantage of all the gaps between how well we think we process information and how well we actually do.

If you're taking in a stream of words, you can stop in the middle and decide, "I don't want to read any further." However, consider what happens when you are confronted with a barrage of images.

Help or hindrance? Health Canada would likely say this reminds people to smoke.

For instance, you see many peripheral visual messages while traveling down a highway or surfing the Web. In both cases, out-of-context messages – whether billboards or banner ads – are intentionally thrown in your path in hopes of catching you unawares. Even more subtle are product placements in movies, or the sugar-coated Web-based "adver-games" for children that actually sell breakfast cereal or toys. It's simply not possible to prefilter all the arriving visual information. Even if you try to ignore one of many simultaneous incoming streams, by the time you recognize undesired images they are often already burned into your memory. And so much of the barrage sticks in your subconscious, unedited, with great power to influence future emotions and decisions.

In the forest, or even on a highway that includes road markings and warning signs, these mechanisms are all helpful for survival, because all that extra input is real and useful. However, consider that 94 percent of the Web sites most popular with Canadian

DOING GOOD

Mervyn Kurlansky first inspired me with his internationalist approach to design when we worked together on an assignment involving the identity for the International Space Station. I learned that Mervyn, born in South Africa, co-founded Pentagram London in 1972. In 1993 he resigned from the storied agency and moved to Denmark where as a prolific author, lecturer, and educator, he has been helping foster worldwide awareness about the designer's global responsibility for over 15 years. He has been involved in numerous projects for the public good. Perhaps most notable is inventing with Sappi Papers the ideas That Matter program: every year since 1999, Sappi has committed $1 million towards the implementation of selected communication campaigns for the social good.

children and teens include marketing materials.[119] I believe that as our society becomes increasingly visually literate, we will reject as abusive this visual overloading designed to deceptively manipulate consumer choice. Until then, as long as professionals continue to engage in this systematic deceit, we drag down both our communities and our spirits.

Some people tell me I should lighten up: that adults have the power and responsibility to decide if they want to respond to ads or not. And frankly, if we are stupid enough to believe that there are two scoops of raisins in every box of Kellogg's Raisin Bran, even though Raisin Bran comes in many sizes of box, it is tempting to declare that we deserve what we get. Indeed, if we had nothing else to think about, if we were all 100 percent healthy, undistracted, and stress-free, and if these messages were presented in a straightforward way one by one, maybe it would be true that we would be poised to take on all the ads we encounter and consider them one by one. But, like so much spam to delete, they wear us down, and intentionally so.

Customer heroes, corporate heroes

When Peter Simons returned to Montréal from a trip to Europe, he had a problem on his hands. The new fall 2008 junior women's fashion catalogue for his La Maison Simons clothing store was in his in-basket, and so were 300 messages from customers upset about the too-thin models being used to appeal to this audience most at risk

for anorexia. The conversation that hit him hardest was from a woman whose bulimic sister had killed herself. When I spoke to Peter the following day, he explained that it took him around 15 minutes to decide to recall the catalogue. Rather than waste more trees, he decided that there would simply be no catalogue that season.

That's a real-life story, with people speaking up to make a difference, and an ethical corporate owner making economically tough and humbling decisions. What will they do differently in the future? "We lost sight of our corporate values, and did harm unnecessarily. We've set a policy on body-mass index for future models. We let down our customers: it won't happen again." We need more like Peter.

Real-time ethics

Imagine that you're a design professional, wrestling with an ethical challenge that has arisen in your work. A client comes to you and says, "Our warehouse is full of widgets we need to sell off and we'd like you to lie in such-and-such a way to get rid of them – and quick." There is bound to be a better way than deception. A creative, ethical solution almost always exists that provides a desirable outcome for both the direct and indirect parties involved.

The direct parties are the direct buyers and sellers (the client, the design firm, and the client's client). The indirect parties to the transaction (remember those externalities?) are the profession, the society, and the environment.

Good design is a strategic, sustainable, ethical response to a business problem. You could come back to that widget manufacturer and say, "Perhaps we could sell a lot of product by telling these white [or not-so-white] lies, but, in the long run, we're going to make you more profit if we speak the truth when selling your product. Plus, we can design a solution that will contribute to your long-term sustainability, as well as that of our agency, our society, and our global environment." If we can't find an appropriate way to package and promote to the intended audience, then perhaps we're seeking the wrong audience. And if we can't find an appropriate audience, then the product itself begs to be redesigned.

In politics, it may be easier to win an election by "swift-boating" the opponent than making credible proposals on how your candidate would improve society if elected, but that does not make it right. Mudslinging robs voters and entire democratic communities of the ability to make informed choices. Similarly, focusing on the frivolous properties of a product distracts consumers from the pertinent information that would put great products in the hands of those that need them.

Adobe pokes fun at themselves: Photoshop has become a mainstream verb

Yes, you will have to think a little harder. It's no coincidence that being forced to think more creatively results in increased innovation.

Yes, it means more time spent on strategy. No problem: I've yet to see a single design project that suffered from too much time spent on strategy. Such time always more than pays for itself in saved time *later* in the process, and of course strategy yields better results. If the client thinks that the strategy is already set, and that you were simply hired to execute, then you can push back and engage them in further strategic discussion. Show what you have to offer.

When the dust clears, you'll be more useful to the client than if you had just blindly said, "Sure, we're happy to play the role you've defined for us in your game." Instead of saying no, you can provide a better version of yes. And you'll find that if you provide your services in that way to clients, over time the fly-by-night clients will disappear, and the clients you *really* want will stick with you.

"But I will lose my job..."

If your employer assigns you work that you are uncomfortable with ethically, you don't have to quit your job; you can respectfully request to be put on another project. Whether uncomfortable with the candidate, the message, or the product, professionals must have the option and the courage to say no to assignments that are not aligned with their ethical principles, whether working for themselves or for someone else. (And subscribing to a code of ethics makes saying no very easy: "I'd love to help you, but it would contravene my professional code of ethics, and of course I can't risk losing my certification: I'm sure you understand.")

In my design firms, designers have always had the option to decline to work on a job with sufficient reason. For instance, if we take on a political project, a designer whose politics contradict the goals of the project can decline to work on it. If you have people working for you, make this choice part of your human resources policy ... before it comes up.

Ultimately, you'll have the clients (or the boss) you deserve.

> "Design creates culture. Culture shapes values. Values determine the future. Design is therefore responsible for the world our children will live in."
>
> ROBERT L. PETERS

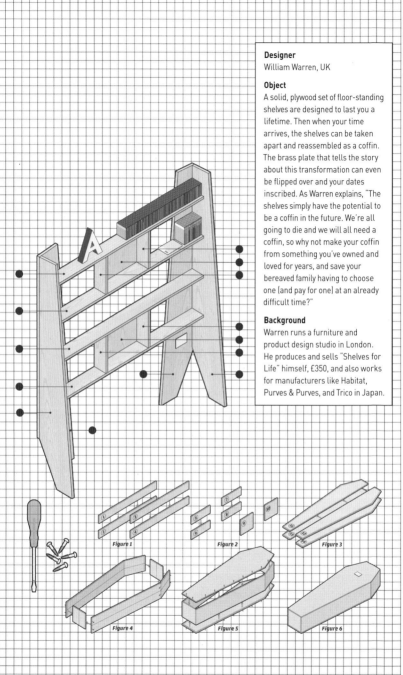

Designer
William Warren, UK

Object
A solid, plywood set of floor-standing shelves are designed to last you a lifetime. Then when your time arrives, the shelves can be taken apart and reassembled as a coffin. The brass plate that tells the story about this transformation can even be flipped over and your dates inscribed. As Warren explains, "The shelves simply have the potential to be a coffin in the future. We're all going to die and we will all need a coffin, so why not make your coffin from something you've owned and loved for years, and save your bereaved family having to choose one (and pay for one) at an already difficult time?"

Background
Warren runs a furniture and product design studio in London. He produces and sells "Shelves for Life" himself, £350, and also works for manufacturers like Habitat, Purves & Purves, and Trico in Japan.

Figure 1

Figure 2

Figure 3

Figure 4

Figure 5

Figure 6

COURTESY RUSSELL BELL AND WALLPAPER

William Warren's "Shelves for Life": re-use to the extreme

> ## "Waste is a design flaw."
> ### KATE KREBS

10 HOW WE DO GOOD IS HOW WE DO GOOD

I'VE ARGUED STRONGLY that sustaining our environment, so that future generations can meet their needs as easily as we can, is the largest challenge in designing a better civilization. Up to this point, we've focused on how our end products can affect global sustainability. However, our process has as much impact as our products. Particularly in a creative industry, the process influences what gets produced, because how we work affects our creative process.

Put more personally: if a designer is who you are, then what you create reflects how you think.

Our creativity makes us innovators in the eyes of our clients: we are opinion leaders when it comes to process. So the next time you pull out a disposable pen at a client briefing, think about this: when ballpoint pens came onto the market right after the Second World War, each cost a very non-disposable $120 (in today's dollars). Before today is done, across five continents, BIC will sell over 14 million ballpoint pens.[120] That's approximately one pen a year for each person on Earth. And that's just BIC. China exports over $1 billion of disposable pens yearly (and in 2008, China also

Landfill waiting to happen

became their largest consumer).[121] Where do all those used pens go? Landfill. And that is where they decompose for 200 to 400 years, after their 6- to 12-month useful life.

It gets worse: BIC states that 13 percent of its hazardous production waste and 29 percent of nonhazardous production waste also ends up in landfill.[122] The products you consume are only the tip of the consumption iceberg: what you hold in your hand is typically only 10 percent of the materials consumed in creating them.[123]

So although recycling helps, you are not avoiding landfill, just delaying it. Meanwhile, if we embrace only recycling as the answer, it becomes the consumer equivalent of tossing back too many low-fat potato chips or sugar-free sodas and thinking that alone will make you healthier.

So jot this down: make a better impression at your next meeting with a classy, nondisposable pen. A refillable Parker that reflects your personality and wardrobe carries a 50-year guarantee. (But my favorite is the Fisher Space Pen black bullet: tiny, elegant, and writes underwater!)

That's a complex load of baggage for one little pen, and that's the point: as professionals, we should pick up each object and reflect on the choices it represents.   *so... I need a refillable Sharpie? yup.*

Second nature: embracing sustainable design practices

Designers must embrace sustainable practices specific to design work (think paperless proofing) as well as green procedures that would apply to any office (think paperless invoicing).

The printing industry is the third largest waste producer on Earth. And almost half of mailed material is trashed without being opened.

The specifics of sustainable design practice are shifting very quickly (and positively). It is unwise to try to describe this moving target of paper composition, vegetable inks, and "waste miles" in print (instead see the online link later in this chapter to take you to some specifics).

"The frog does not drink up the pond in which she lives." BUDDHIST PROVERB

What is not in flux are these three points of good news:

1. Sustainable practices won't take any more time than what you do now, once you are familiar with them.
2. Sustainable practices will, on balance, save money for both you and your clients.
3. You don't have to do it all at once. Try one thing on your next project. Then once you've mastered that, try another, and so on... (If you must be intimidated, I'd rather it be by this fourth truth: sustainable design practice will rapidly become the standard. If you don't learn this stuff, you are going to be left behind.)

COURTESY THOMAS.MATTHEWS

Your Ocean is a permanent maritime gallery constructed entirely from reclaimed, recycled, and sustainable materials

Climate change campaign for schools in the UK

DOING GOOD

Dinner with Sophie Thomas of London's thomas.matthews the night before she keynotes on sustainable design at a European design conference unearths two truths: we are both children of activists, and she is obsessed with waste. She was distracted by the huge expenditure of resources involved in flying to a conference. Sophie and Kristin Matthews founded their firm in 1998 to practice good design built on sustainable principles. Back then, the focus was still on Reduce, Recycle, Reuse; before the agenda became larger and the challenge more acute. Her mission is now to share their process: the designer as social change agent. In 2008, she invented a sustainability slideshow to run at the London Design Festival called "greengaged," which can be attached to any design conference.

For instance, here's something to try in your next proposal: include an optional line item to cover the cost of making the entire project carbon-neutral (or even better, carbon-positive). We have yet to encounter a client who found this choice distasteful.

If you're not already aware of the details of sustainable and universal design practices, get educated.

Most importantly, all professionals need to learn about the triple bottom line: people, planet, profit. This has become the dominant approach to full-cost accounting: it expands traditional accounting reporting to include social and environmental corporate performance alongside financial performance. Sustainable design is good economics. We need to apply the triple bottom line to our own business plans, as well as the success measures for every project.

If you'd like to take it up one another notch, consider a quadruple bottom line model, where we add cultural sustainability to the mix. One could argue that it is our ability to design and inherit culture that differentiates us most from all other species.

Once you've educated yourself about sustainable practices, practice injecting such ideas into every project and procedure until it becomes second nature.

Strive to surround yourself only with well-designed reusable, sustainable products and processes.

If you are already up to speed on how, then help spread that know-how and habit by example, and perhaps even push the envelope (a reused envelope of course!) of what is acceptable in your community.

Visit www.davidberman.com/dogood for an evergreened list of resources and groups in our community that are developing sustainable practices you can start to implement right away.

Eight Top Tips for Buying Sustainable Design

1

Insist that every project starts with a written strategy,
whose measurable objectives include a triple or quadruple bottom line.

2

Choose designers (certified ones, if available)
who have made a public commitment to minimum standards of performance and
social responsibility, and that will keep you informed of what's new.

3

Plan products that will be designed to last, and will be designed for all.

4

Consider solutions that start with eco-friendly materials
(preferably from nearby, ethical suppliers) that reuse existing things, or that result
in things that can be reused (or at least recycled).

5

Offset any unavoidable carbon footprint of your project.

6

If you can't find a promise to make about your product that you'd feel comfortable
making to your children or best friend, redesign your product.

7

Tell the world about your great process:
lead by example, and take the credit you deserve.

8

Don't just do good work, do good.

I MAKE BEAUTIFUL TRASH

PHOTO: EREN BUTLER

Designers around the world are recognizing their power and their responsibility

"Thoughts are mightier than armies. Principles have achieved more victories than horsemen or chariots."

WILLIAM MILLER PAXTON (1824–1904)

11 PROFESSIONAL CLIMATE CHANGE

SPRINKLED THROUGHOUT this book are stories of individuals from the design world making a difference to the whole world. Why not you too?

There is no reason why you cannot also make an extraordinary mark in our world. You simply have to decide to do it. You don't need to be the greatest that ever lived at what you do: I am certainly no all-star, and neither are most of the individuals whose contributions I celebrate in this book (sorry, pals!).

Einstein's brain may have been a bit larger than most, and Michael Jordan is certainly taller, however most people who have left the world an exceptional legacy are people just like you who simply decided to do the extraordinary. If, like most people, you need some kind of green light or permission to behave in an extraordinary way, I am hereby giving you permission to be extraordinary.

Organizational change is also afoot in our industries: each time, it starts with one person. This chapter highlights hopeful examples of leading steps creative thinkers are taking as the global momentum of doing good takes hold.

PHOTO: DAVID BERMAN

On display at MOMA New York, paraSITE by Michael Rakowitz: transportable homeless shelter, made from discarded materials, inflated by warm neighborly outtake ducts.

First things first

The idea that designers' talents should be directed beyond selling stuff is not new: in 1964, Ken Garland released the *First Things First* manifesto in London, signed by 22 concerned designers.

In 2005, during our tour of downtown London, Ken's wife Wanda showed me the McDonald's restaurant that used to be London's city hall: it dawned on me that poor countries are not the only ones at risk of having their cultures ground up and loaded with filler.

For me, Ken exemplifies the designer who is both ordinary and extraordinary. That evening, over tea in Ken's Camden home-studio, he reminisced that he wasn't suggesting we should have any less fun; he simply thought that our skills could be used in much nobler ways.

See Appendix A to read the entire manifesto

A manifesto

We, the undersigned, are graphic designers, photographers and students who have been brought up in a world in which the techniques and apparatus of advertising have persistently been presented to us as the most lucrative, effective and desirable means of using our talents. We have been bombarded with publications devoted to this belief, applauding the work of those who have flogged their skill and imagination to sell such things as:

cat food, stomach powders, detergent, hair restorer, striped toothpaste, aftershave lotion, beforeshave lotion, slimming diets, fattening diets, deodorants, fizzy water, cigarettes, roll-ons, pull-ons and slip-ons.

By far the greatest time and effort of those working in the advertising industry are wasted on these trivial purposes, which contribute little or nothing to our national prosperity.

In common with an increasing number of the general public, we have reached a saturation point at which the high pitched scream of consumer selling is no more than sheer noise. We think that there are other things more worth using our skill and experience on. There are signs for streets and buildings, books and periodicals, catalogues, instructional manuals, industrial photography, educational aids, films, television features, scientific and industrial publications and all the other media through which we promote our trade, our education, our culture and our greater awareness of the world.

We do not advocate the abolition of high pressure consumer advertising: this is not feasible. Nor do we want to take any of the fun out of life. But we are proposing a reversal of priorities in favour of the more useful and more lasting forms of communication. We hope that our

society will tire of gimmick merchants, status salesmen and hidden persuaders, and that the prior call on our skills will be for worthwhile purposes. With this in mind, we propose to share our experience and opinions, and to make them available to colleagues, students and others who may be interested.

Edward Wright
Geoffrey White
William Slack
Caroline Rawlence
Ian McLaren
Sam Lambert
Ivor Kamlish
Gerald Jones
Bernard Higton
Brian Grimbly
John Garner
Ken Garland
Anthony Froshaug
Robin Fior
Germano Facetti
Ivan Dodd
Harriet Crowder
Anthony Clift
Gerry Cinamon
Robert Chapman
Ray Carpenter
Ken Briggs

Published by Ken Garland, 13 Oakley Sq N.W.1
Printed by Goodwin Press Ltd. London N.4

COURTESY KEN GARLAND

Designers united, designers taking responsibility

In 1983, the world bodies of the main design disciplines (Icograda, IFI, and icsid)[124] jointly declared that "a designer accepts professional responsibility to act in the best interest of ecology and of the natural environment."

In the year 2000, the Society of Graphic Designers of Canada adopted a courageous and progressive national code of ethics, standing on the shoulders of inspiring documents from around the world. I'm proud to say that our resulting code went further than any other code that we were aware of from any profession: it established, by definition, that professionalism includes a commitment to social and environmental responsibility.

Icograda, the world body for communication design, offers the Canadian model as a benchmark for design associations in other countries seeking to establish their own codes of conduct.

In 2005, AIGA, the world's largest national association of designers, adopted our language when republishing its own professional standards, then in 2008 translated it for use in design education in China. Also in 2008, we helped Norway adapt the Canadian policy to serve as its first code of ethics for Norwegian graphic designers and illustrators.

See Appendix B to read highlights of the Canadian code

Meanwhile, design associations around the world have been injecting environmental and social responsibility into their codes, from Ukraine to Australia to Israel to Brazil.

Certifying graphic designers

Since 1996, in my home province of Ontario, Canada, graphic design has been a certified profession – in no small part due to the heroic efforts of one Toronto designer named Albert Ng. The term "R.G.D." (and "Registered Graphic Designer") is now a professional

DOING GOOD   In the 1980s, Karen Blincoe was making a good living as a designer in London, creating signage for tennis championships and packaging for supermarket chains. An assignment photographing toxically-produced fake fruit in a deceptively natural setting made her ask herself what she was really doing with her best professional years. So, in 1991, she established the International Centre for Creativity, Innovation and Sustainability in a thatched-roof farmhouse in Denmark's northern Zealand. At ICIS, she invented a system of masterclasses where international experts lead interdisciplinary lectures, discussions, debate, and group work. In 2003, I was privileged to lead a masterclass: the group of young Danish designers seemed poised to lead the Danish design industry for the next generation.

designation protected by law, just like "registered nurse" or "medical doctor" or "lawyer." This was a first in the Americas and second in the world. Designers from across Canada worked to get the certification in place.

To receive this title, you must pass an examination, a quarter of which evaluates knowledge of professional conduct standards. The curriculum of Ontario design schools has been adjusted to prepare graduates to pass that exam.

As the president of the first elected board of this association, I worked hard to craft bylaws that include a professional commitment to society and the environment. The *Rules of Professional Conduct* are linked through certification to the law of Ontario: designers can lose their designation through a formal grievance procedure that any citizen can initiate.

PHOTO: CYNTHIA HOFFOS

Certification is a force of good that is not exclusionary. It doesn't stop anyone from designing. It doesn't limit creativity. But it does recognize the fundamental role that designers now hold within society. And it's a huge step towards our society recognizing that not just anyone should be entrusted with crafting critical visual messaging or products.

Certification does not guarantee that a design buyer will get an all-star designer. It *does* establish a minimum standard: those who hire designers get a person bound to a minimum level of performance with respect to business procedures, education, skill, and ethical behavior. Certification helps protect society from the damages of predatory persuasion and exploitative design; much the same way that certification of architects protects us against buildings that could fall down on people.

Ontario is not unique: there is also a form of graphic design certification in Switzerland. And in 2008, Norway adopted their own form of certification for graphic designers. Meanwhile, Canadian designers outside Ontario continue to explore adoption of the construct in other provinces.

I've lectured on certification in the United States, Hungary, the Czech Republic, and Colombia because I believe strongly that certification is part of the solution: if you need help making it happen where you live, we can work together to get it done.

Colombian students volunteered to work towards certification for designers in their country

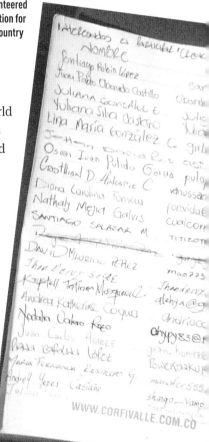

Global movement

In 1999, activating the brainchild of Japanese designer Kenji Ekuan, the world bodies for the main design disciplines (graphic design, industrial design, and interior design) birthed Design for the World, a joint organization dedicated to global social responsibility, in conjunction with the Barcelona Design Center. Here's the idea: Meet with the global nongovernment organizations working in the front lines of need (UN High Commission for Refugees, International Red Cross, Médecins Sans Frontières, etc.) to determine how design can help those in greatest need. Then match up volunteer designers to craft

PHOTO: DAVID BERMAN

PHOTO: DAVID BERMAN

Rethinking: Hong Kong Design Centre held a social responsibility themed design week, right down to the cotton bags. Cirque du Soleil chops up used tents, using local labor to make shoulder bags.

solutions, funded by corporations that have agreed to fulfill their social responsibility mandates this way. It remains to fulfill its potential.

Better design events

Designers must educate the public that design is about strategy, not decoration. However, such attempts are repeatedly undermined by a design world hooked on competitions and awards ceremonies that celebrate only creativity instead of strategy results and sustainability.

A little bored during a national GDC board meeting in Nova Scotia, Victoria's Peggy Cady and I started to brainstorm: how about a design competition that celebrates the best results to the community, rather than the best creativity or technical skill? I've only known Peggy as a person of action. Within a year, the Victoria chapter of the Graphic Designers of Canada had

PHOTOS: DAVID BERMAN

Design Cares exhibit in Hong Kong

Inequality Matters exhibit in Beijing

produced the Design Cares competition. I was to speak at the opening of the exhibit, and was awestruck immediately when entering the room. Members of the public and media from the city of Victoria, British Columbia, wandered from exhibit to exhibit, immersed in how design was doing good in their community: in their hospitals, in their streets, in their water, in their air. Design mattered. Unmistakably. The event was so popular that it resulted in a traveling exhibition that has toured four continents.

Another example of a design show that matters, the massive Inequality Matters posters illustrate how much disparity there is in the world regarding the human condition. The original series was designed by Tom Geismar through AIGA for the 2005 World Summit, the largest gathering of the world's leaders to date.

And in Icograda, we have recently developed global policy for greener events, to help designers lead by example.

Designing for all

"Good design enables, bad design disables." So declares the 2004 Stockholm Declaration of EIDD – Design For All Europe, which has chapters in twenty countries. EIDD is dedicated to how design can improve life while leaving no one behind. Sweden's Finn Petrén, EIDD's president, explained to me that being "accessible" is not enough, because that term suggests that material is simply available to all. EIDD demands design that at a minimum enables an equivalently immersive and convenient experience for all, regardless of age, culture, or ability. They lobby all levels of government, professionals, and businesses.

Truly inclusive design isn't just a moral imperative. The majority of humans, at one point in their lives, will have some significant

"Everyone has the right freely to participate in the cultural life of the community, to enjoy the arts and to share in scientific advancement and its benefits."
ARTICLE 27.1, UNIVERSAL DECLARATION OF HUMAN RIGHTS, 1948

disability. Thus, from information technology to packaging to tourism, designing for all is not just kind, it's good business.

As I mentioned earlier, it was fairly early on in the Internet's development that accessibility was recognized as a driver. The World Wide Web Consortium, housed at MIT and led by Sir Tim Berners-Lee, has published the 2.0 release of its Web Content Accessibility Guidelines. Accessibility has been a Web priority since the 1990s, with the realization of how liberating the Internet is for the hundreds of millions of people worldwide who have permanent or temporary disabilities or challenges.

Canada's federal government lead the world in the speed and depth to which it embraced an accessible Web experience for its audience: something I've been very proud to be a part of. Simply put, Web pages that are not accessible for people with disabilities and difficulties are not allowed to be posted anywhere in the federal government's Web presence. This policy has been in effect since 2002.

First things next

Design critic Max Bruinsma believes that writers and designers are akin, in that both organize interfaces between content and form. "Designers are cultural agents," he explained over midnight grappa at Turin's Design Week. I asked him, out of all the design literature he has worked with throughout his career, what is he most proud of? He said that without a doubt it was working with Kalle Lasn and Rick Poynor on the second release of the *First Things First* manifesto, when he was editor of *Eye* magazine. A decade later he stills gets a substantial amount of e-mail about *First Things First 2000*. *Adbusters* magazine led the charge to release a year 2000 version of the *First*

Things First manifesto, this time signed by designers from around the world, including Ken. It was jointly published in *Adbusters*, the *AIGA Journal*, *Blueprint*, *Émigré*, *Eye*, *Form*, and *Items*. Kalle reflected to me recently that "in 2000, the world still looked fairly benign. Since then the triple punch of psychological, geopolitical, and environmental upheaval is causing designers to wake up."

The rereleased manifesto calls out "in expectation that no more decades will pass before it is taken to heart." Now is our time to take up its call.

Massive change happens

Waiting for change can be painful; however, when change does come, it often arrives with shocking speed. It took less than 15 years for the use of recycled paper to become the norm, rather than the exception. Ninety percent of Europe's top companies now publish corporate social responsibility reports (and the majority of the top 100 U.S. companies do, too).[125] And after years of frustratingly slow adoption, being green has now become a mainstream obsession.

This postcard is distributed at events where the Dalai Lama speaks in Canada

so: gonna keep this in the Chinese edition?

For many people who want to challenge the existing system, the only choices are to either protest injustice or to work from outside the system. But with the creative, collaborative, and persuasive power and opportunities of today's professional, one can likely have a far greater and more lasting impact by changing the system from within.

It is clear that the change we need has already started to take place, on every continent where humans create stuff.

"But what can *I* do right now?" you may ask. Well, for starters, you can turn the page.

PHOTO: DAVID BERMAN

CONSUMERS OF DESIGN:

SHOPPING TIPS FOR AGENTS OF SOCIAL CHANGE

Temporary installation to draw media attention to the UK launch of International No Shop Day: shop posters were screenprinted over recycled billboards. The language of shopping – shop fronts, sales coupons, receipts, and shopping bags – forms a No Shop brand, turning consumerism on its head.

COURTESY THOMAS.MATTHEWS

Have a personal mission. **Rethink.** Know what you need, then seek out products that will fit you for a long time. **Read *Cradle To Cradle*.** Demand objects that are designed to last. **Avoid disposables.** Carry one great pen. **Carry chopsticks.** Carry your own shopping bag. **Carry a tune.** Be happy with your hair. **Give ideas as presents more often, things less often.** Give a gift subscription to *Adbusters*. **Eat less junk.** Eat fewer animals. **Avoid bottled water.** Drink local beer. **Seek simple entertainment.** Have fun. **Remember that you are already beautiful (and embrace those who have told you so).** Avoid style magazines: fashion is declawed rebellion, and a weak substitute at that. **Entertain yourself simply.** Don't leave your car idling. **If you don't have democracy, fight for it.** If you do have democracy, fight to keep it. **Then vote for lawmakers who will make laws that control visual lies and will regulate products that steal dreams.** Shake off the excessive amount of stuff you have in your life, then see how much lighter you feel. **Plan more carefully,** so you can consume more efficiently. **Resist all messages that seek to convince you that you need to consume in order to feel good.** If shopping is your hobby, find a more sustainable hobby. **If shopping is your habit, figure out why.** Avoid products made of PVC, the hazardous waste of the display industry. **Buy products that tell the truth.** Resist designer products unless you see the value the designer has contributed. **Resist being manipulated by visual lies.** Resist giving up your mental environment to corporations that wish to post billboards in your mind. **Don't get too comfy.** Stay alert. **Demand truth.** Share your truth. **Speak out when you see visual lies.** Think about how we can apply the principles in this book to all professions. **Lead by example.** Teach it. **Live it.** Share it. **Design your better future, then help us all design ours.**

"Be the change you want to see in the world."

MAHATMA GANDHI (1869–1948)

the do good

The time
to commit
is now.

IMMEDIACY

1

"I will be
true to my
profession."

ETHICS

pledge

2 PRINCIPLES — "I will be true to myself."

3 EFFORT — "I will spend at least 10 percent of my professional time helping repair the world."

"Don't just do good design, do good."
DAVID BERMAN

Award-winning ad for cosmetic surgery: but aren't our noses good enough already?

"Now that we can do anything, what will we do?" BRUCE MAU

12 "WHAT CAN ~~ONE~~ ANY PROFESSIONAL DO?" *Commit!*

EVERYBODY: Please read this final chapter. Think about how these principles apply to your work even if you do not call yourself a designer.

Imagine what would be possible if we did not participate in the export of overconsumption and the unbridled fulfillment of greed. No one understands the powerful mechanism behind these manipulations better than design professionals, and we all have the creativity and persuasiveness to make a positive change. We must act, we must be heard ... and sometimes we must simply say no by designing a better yes.

Some choose to pursue design purely as an exercise in the aesthetic. I know that simply creating beautiful objects or surrounding yourself with beautifully designed things can help create a fulfilling and comfortable life. However, that is only the surface of the potential good and sense of accomplishment you can achieve with creative skills.

Go further: recognize the interdependence, power, and influence of your role as a professional, and let it resonate with the world around you and within you.

People of all professions ask me, "So what can *I* do?" My answer: take this three-part pledge, with its components of professionalism, personal responsibility, and time.

"I will be true to my profession."

For a couple of millennia now, doctors have been taking a pledge. Imagine if, instead of following the Hippocratic Oath, doctors had only focused on the wealth to be had from cosmetic surgery... or shaking down dying people for their entire inheritance in exchange for a remedy that would extend life by a few weeks.

Design professionals have built their own oaths. Join a national or regional association of professionals that has a code of ethics (sometimes known as standards or rules of professional conduct).

Your professional association should have a code of ethics that includes a commitment to social responsibility (and many other good things: licensing, authorship, competitions...). If not, use Icograda's template or call me: we'll work together to get that remedied.

If there isn't such an organization in your region, you can start one (we can help!), become a Friend of Icograda, or become a member at large of a professional organization in a nearby region (such as AIGA).

By joining, you'll have made a public professional commitment to abide to a minimum standard of ethical conduct. (Of course there will be many other benefits to joining as well.)

A commitment to professional ethics implies a minimum standard of conduct: a combination of your personal and public principles. The personal commitment you make to yourself, in the form of your mission, morals, and beliefs. The professional commitment is a promise to uphold a common set of published minimum standards of behavior, which you make when you join a professional body. Professionalism implies a 24/7 commitment, a recognition that your profession is part of who you are.

[You can go further as well: there are issue-specific professional credos that you can commit to regarding particular issues within your field. Here are some examples from the design profession:
• the Design Can Change pledge at www.designcanchange.org
• the Designers Accord at www.designersaccord.org
• Catherine Morley's No-Spec site at www.no-spec.com
…or visit www.davidberman.com/dogood for a longer list.]

"I will be true to myself."

Be guided by what you know is right.

People ask me what constitutes doing good. I can't answer for you whether a hybrid SUV is part of the solution or part of the problem. However, I do know that if all professionals simply looked into their hearts, chose to be their best selves, and did only work that was in alignment with their principles, we'd be 90 percent there.

Be aware of your principles. Part of what designers do as professionals – just as is expected of doctors, judges, or engineers –

is to strive to maintain one's principles all the time. So when it comes to the question of what is right or wrong in the professional world, simply ask yourself, "How would I deal with this on a personal level? Would I recommend this product to my children? Could I look my daughter or my best friend in the eye while speaking this message or pitching the product or idea I've created, or would I have to look away?"

I don't have all the answers. I do know that if each one of us forbids ourselves from doing anything or helping to say anything that is out of alignment with our personal principles, then that will be more than enough to change the world.

Saying no at times is a big part of it. But it is often more powerful to propose an alternative solution that aligns with the principles of all parties. If we all do that, we'll get the shift required: we'll be contributing more than we're taking away; doing more good than harm.

"This is your life, and it's ending one minute at a time."

TYLER DURDEN

3 "I will spend at least 10 percent of my professional time helping repair the world."

I am not asking you to sell your firm. I am not asking you to quit your job. I am not asking you to work pro bono (well, maybe a little bit, but that's another story).

Here is what I am asking...

Christians call it a tithe. Muslims have something similar: *zakat*. Jews call it *ma'aser*. For the Chinese, it is *ci shan*.

And since time is money, I'm asking that you commit 10 percent of your professional time to help repair the world.

That's four hours of a 40-hour professional work week (and I'm clearly giving you a break here by pretending that you only work a 40-hour week). Four hours of design for an organization, a company, or government clearly acting for the social good.

There are close to 2 million designers in the world.[126] If each were to take just 10 percent of their professional time, imagine what would be possible. Close to 8 million hours a week of designing a more just, more sustainable, more caring civilization.

"When I retire from Madison Avenue, I am going to
start a secret society of masked vigilantes who will
travel the world on motor bicycles, chopping down
posters at the dark of the moon."

DAVID OGILVY, FOUNDER OF OGILVY & MATHER (1911–1999)

Make money doing it.

Let me be clear: I am *not* asking you to work for free. I am simply
asking you to make sure that at least four hours of each professional
week is spent on projects that are socially just.

When I sold my design agency, and decided to rededicate myself
to working on projects that matter while sharing what I know, I
expected to take a pay cut. I was surprised to discover that working
exclusively for clients who are doing good in the world actually pays
well. I suspect it is because they have products and services that
truly fulfill on their promises. And clients like that tend to be stable
and healthy organizations that also value my ethical practices. I also
know that when I am working with integrity, I produce better work.

Sometimes it's a bit of a Robin Hood thing: the wealthier clients,
who get to be the most demanding, effectively subsidize the less-
wealthy clients, who allow us more creative and deadline flexibility.
It's healthy cross-pollination that nurtures everyone involved.

Now.

Are we too late? Not at all. The time is perfect. Because of the
increasing visual literacy and networking in our society, I believe we
can design a scenario where we avoid running the ship aground.
15 years ago, if you said you were a designer, people asked, "What is
that?" Today, they tend to already know. Instead they are now
asking, "What are designers really about? Are they tradespeople?

Are they craftspeople? Are they artists? Professionals? Are they ethical? How can I think like a designer?" What's our answer going to be? It seems the perfect time to be able to declare, "We're about this, and we're definitely not about that."

If not now, then when? I was invited to speak on ethics at one of the largest design schools in the U.S., Virginia Commonwealth University in Richmond – the heart of Tobacco Country. The talk was mandatory for design students, and in a huge campus auditorium I made a point of using example after example from the cigarette industry. When it was over, I wasn't sure if I'd be shown the door or embraced. After the Q&A, a student came up to me and said, "Thank you so much. I'm from a tobacco family, and until today I assumed I'd be taking a job in the tobacco industry."

Young designers often promise me they'll change: later, once they've established themselves and gotten a foothold in the industry. More experienced designers will tell me that they wish I would have reached them years ago, but that right now they have a mortgage and kids to feed: they claim the right time will be "someday." I tell both younger and older designers the same thing: our time is now.

"It is only with the heart that one can see rightly. What is most important is invisible to the eye." THE LITTLE PRINCE

commit

DOING GOOD
sidebar? I've had many audiences raise their hands to commit to give a percentage of their time to repairing the world. You'll recall the ICIS masterclass from an earlier "Doing Good" sidebar? The participants one-upped me by applying strength in numbers. Lene Vad Jensen is one of the founders of the group that the masterclass participants formed, called Designers Of Today. DOT is a multidisciplinary forum of 30 designers who formally donate 5 percent of their professional design hours for "Design to improve life." For example, DOT offered 5 percent of their combined time for a year to UNICEF: a block worth more than $200,000. They turned UNICEF's global warehouse in Denmark into a learning showroom for all visitors, and planned a game that teachers can instantly use to teach children's rights.

"All we have to decide is what to do with the time that is given us." GANDALF

Are you ready to take the Do Good Pledge?

Each one of us has a choice: We can spend the best years of our careers helping to convince people they don't belong, that they don't smell right, that they're not thin enough or famous enough or tall enough or red enough or white enough or rich enough or smooth enough... and all they have to do to belong is to satisfy manufactured needs by buying more stuff.

Or we can remember that we all belong, and that each of us has an important role in working together, making the world better.

What design will be about is now up to us.

Design is a very young profession, without a long history that's impossible to uproot. We've barely begun. The role of design need not be defined by selling ideas and things through deceit.

Over 95 percent of all designers who have ever lived are alive today.

Together, it is up to us to decide what role design will play. Is it going to be about selling sugar water and smoke and mirrors to the vulnerable child within every one of us ... or helping to repair the world?

It should be about embracing a responsible and honored role in society – as it is with medical doctors, lawyers, and engineers. Society will then truly recognize the power of design, and the special role that design and design thinking will play in a brighter future.

I know that if we fulfill the gifts of our professional skills by recognizing our power and the stewardship responsibility that accompanies that power, we can make a real difference. And since we can, we must.

Perhaps 100,000 lifetimes of human history preceded yours, and hopefully at least more than that will follow. Do you ever wonder why your life is taking place right now, at this remarkable turning point in human history? I know that we can continue to work together to create an environment where our children and our children's children will be able to fulfill their needs as easily as we are able to today. The future for humanity lies in the decisions we will make in our lifetimes.

The past 6,000 years has been civilization's collective childhood. From here on, it's one civilization for all – or not. So in this post-Darwinian world, it's up to us: the product designers, the message designers, the design thinkers, the specialists in the transportation of things and ideas over great distances and time. We must make sure that our inventions are not just clever but also wise; that they don't just do cool stuff, but are also in alignment with a sustainable future for humanity.

And, should civilization survive and thrive, perhaps 100,000 years from now people will look back at this "teenagehood" of civilization and admire the legacy of how we chose to spend our creative energies ... of the ideas we chose to propagate.

So choose well: **don't just do good design, do good.**

We need you:
Take the Do Good Pledge right now.

Go to www.davidberman.com/dogood

www.davidberman.com/dogood

DOING GOOD

Do you know of someone doing good (such as yourself)? Please visit www.davidberman.com/dogood and tell us what they've done.

Act now.

I meant it. If you haven't taken the Do Good Pledge, visit www.davidberman.com/dogood and do it now.

Read more, do more.

Go further: visit www.davidberman.com/dogood for recommendations of books and Web sites to visit, and for more things you can do.

PHOTO: KHADIJA SAFRI

APPENDIX A
FIRST THINGS FIRST MANIFESTO

A manifesto by Ken Garland, London, 1964

We, the undersigned, are graphic designers, photographers and students who have been brought up in a world in which the techniques and apparatus of advertising have persistently been presented to us as the most lucrative, effective and desirable means of using our talents. We have been bombarded with publications devoted to this belief, applauding the work of those who have flogged their skill and imagination to sell such things as: cat food, stomach powders, detergent, hair restorer, striped toothpaste, aftershave lotion, beforeshave lotion, slimming diets, fattening diets, deodorants, fizzy water, cigarettes, roll-ons, pull-ons and slip-ons.

By far the greatest effort of those working in the advertising industry are wasted on these trivial purposes, which contribute little or nothing to our national prosperity.

In common with an increasing number of the general public, we have reached a saturation point at which the high pitched scream of consumer selling is no more than sheer noise. We think that there are other things more worth using our skill and experience on. There are signs for streets and buildings, books and periodicals, catalogues, instructional manuals, industrial photography, educational aids, films, television features, scientific and industrial publications and all the other media through which we promote our trade, our education, our culture and our greater awareness of the world.

We do not advocate the abolition of high pressure consumer advertising: this is not feasible. Nor do we want to take any of the fun out of life. But we are proposing a reversal of priorities in favour of the more useful and more lasting forms of communication. We hope that our society will tire of gimmick merchants, status salesmen and hidden persuaders, and that the prior call on our skills will be for worthwhile purposes. With this in mind we propose to share our experience and opinions, and to make them available to colleagues, students and others who may be interested.

APPENDIX B
EXCERPT FROM THE GDC'S *CODE OF ETHICS*

Here are highlights from the 2000 *Code of Ethics*
of the Society of Graphic Designers of Canada
(GDC). These same clauses are mirrored in the
Rules of Professional Conduct of the Association of
Registered Graphic Designers of Ontario, and
thus became linked to the laws of Ontario:

Responsibility to Society and the Environment

31. A Member, while engaged in the practice or
    instruction of graphic design, shall not do or fail
    to do anything that constitutes a deliberate or
    reckless disregard for the health and safety of the
    communities in which they live and practise or the
    privacy of the individuals and businesses therein.
    Members shall take a responsible role in the visual
    portrayal of people, the consumption of natural resources,
    and the protection of animals and the environment.

32. A Member shall not accept instructions from a client or employer that
    involve infringement of another person's or group's human rights or
    property rights without permission of such other person or group, or
    consciously act in any manner involving any such infringement.

33. A Member shall not make use of goods or services offered by
    manufacturers, suppliers or contractors that are accompanied by an
    obligation that is detrimental to the best interests of his or her client,
    society or the environment.

34. A Member shall not display a lack of knowledge, skill or judgment or
    disregard for the public or the environment of a nature or to an extent
    that demonstrates that the Member is unfit to be a Member of the
    Society of Graphic Designers of Canada.

35. A Member shall not contract directly with the client of his or her client
    or employer without obtaining the permission of his or her client or
    employer to do so.

APPENDIX C
EXCERPT FROM AIGA'S *STANDARDS OF PROFESSIONAL PRACTICE*

A professional designer adheres to principles of integrity that demonstrate respect for the profession, for colleagues, for clients, for audiences or consumers, and for society as a whole.

AIGA Standards of
Professional Practice

AIGA encourages the highest level of professional conduct
in design. These standards reflect conduct that is in
the best interest of the profession, clients and the public.

AIGA

The designer's responsibility to the public

6.1 A professional designer shall avoid projects that will result in harm to the public.

6.2 A professional designer shall communicate the truth in all situations and at all times; his or her work shall not make false claims nor knowingly misinform. A professional designer shall represent messages in a clear manner in all forms of communication design and avoid false, misleading and deceptive promotion.

6.3 A professional designer shall respect the dignity of all audiences and shall value individual differences even as they avoid depicting or stereotyping people or groups of people in a negative or dehumanizing way. A professional designer shall strive to be sensitive to cultural values and beliefs, and engage in fair and balanced communication design that fosters and encourages mutual understanding.

The designer's responsibility to society and the environment

7.1 A professional designer, while engaged in the practice or instruction of design, shall not knowingly do or fail to do anything that constitutes a deliberate or reckless disregard for the health and safety of the communities in which he or she lives and practices or the privacy of the individuals and businesses therein. A professional designer shall take a responsible role in the visual portrayal of people, the consumption of natural resources, and the protection of animals and the environment.

7.2 A professional designer shall not knowingly accept instructions from a client or employer that involve infringement of another person's or group's human rights or property rights without permission of such other person or group, or consciously act in any manner involving any such infringement.

7.3 A professional designer shall not knowingly make use of goods or services offered by manufacturers, suppliers or contractors that are accompanied by an obligation that is substantively detrimental to the best interests of his or her client, society or the environment.

7.4 A professional designer shall refuse to engage in or countenance discrimination on the basis of race, sex, age, religion, national origin, sexual orientation or disability.

7.5 A professional designer shall strive to understand and support the principles of free speech, freedom of assembly, and access to an open marketplace of ideas and shall act accordingly.

APPENDIX D
THE ROAD TO NORWAY AND CHINA

Okay, first of all, thank you for reading this far: I mean who reads appendices?

There is no English translation for the *Grafills Etiske Retningslinjer*. If you would like to read it in Norwegian, please visit www.grafill.no and find it there.

Speaking of Norway and how many small acts can build up to making a significant difference in the world, I promised back on page 8 to tell you the end of the scooter story.

Here we go....

You'll recall that, when we last left David, he was on his motor scooter on the way to a meeting, intent on naïvely asking that the local Society of Graphic Designers of Canada chapter make a professional commitment regarding gender issues in specific, and social responsibility in general.

Freshly aware of the untidy nature of graphic design, I parked my scooter in the Byward Market and arrived at the annual general meeting of the Society's Ottawa chapter. At end of the agenda, chapter president Mary Ann Maruska asked for any "Other Business." I stood up and sheepishly read out my manifesto about feminism and ecology and every designer's duty. First, the owner of one of the larger agencies in town responded saying that we designers just follow clients' orders; that the content is not the fault of the designers. Lots of heads were nodding, and for a moment it looked like my quest would end right there.

Then his wife and business partner spoke up. She said she thought there was something to this: wasn't it up to us to choose what we would or would not participate in? She related that this issue had been bothering her for some time, but she'd never voiced it before. More designers chimed in ... and a heated debate raged for 45 minutes.

Meanwhile, Mary Ann took me aside to explain that what I needed to change was the *Code of Ethics*. That had to be done nationally, and the place to start was in the local chapter – she was an excellent recruiter!

The next year, I found myself vice-president of the local chapter, while Mary Ann moved on to join the national executive.

When Mary Ann became national president, she lovingly lured me into setting up a national committee to work on the *Code of Ethics* with Robert L. Peters of Manitoba (who would go on to be a president of Icograda), pointing out that this would give me the opportunity to insert my ideas. And so the drafting began. By 1998, with the help of committed GDC leaders from across Canada, we had drafted a *Code of Ethics* for designers in Canada which recognized our responsibility to society and the environment.

Meanwhile, certification for Ontario designers was afoot in Canada. In a meeting in Toronto, Albert Ng and Rod Nash asked if I would be willing to run for the presidency of the first elected Board of the Association of Registered Graphic Designers of Ontario. "No way," said I: already GDC vice-president now, and working on many other good projects; it was the last thing I wanted. He then pointed out that, as president, I could draft the bylaws of the first professional association of certified graphic designers in the world outside of Switzerland, and that would naturally include *Rules of Professional Conduct*, which could include my code of ethics clauses. Hmm... okay: I agreed and served as president from 1997 through 1999.

In 1999, those *Rules of Professional Conduct* were legally vetted in Ontario, and bound to the laws of the province. In 2000, almost identical language was adopted nationally by the GDC. In 2001, Icograda, the world body for design, adopted the Canadian code as a template to be offered to other national bodies seeking to create their own.

Meanwhile, the GDC made me a Fellow for my work on both the code and certification for designers, which is likely what brought me to the attention of Mervyn Kurlansky, president of Icograda, who convinced me to join the board of that world body.

At the opening of Canada's hosting of the world headquarters for Icograda in Montreal in May 2005, organizers asked me to speak later that year about professional ethics in Norway and Denmark at the Era 05 world design congress. They wanted to know about made-in-Canada design professionalism.

During the talk in Oslo, I threw down a challenge to the Norwegians: about having a code of ethics, and making it stick through government-sponsored certification. And a few people (and as we know, it only takes a few...) took it very seriously. Later that year, they contacted me about working from the Canadian template. Not long after, at a meeting in Hong Kong in 2006, AIGA executive director Richard Grefé asked me if we could together work the Canadian clauses into the Americans' revised *Standards of Professional Practice.*

Then, early in 2008, Grafill, the Norwegian association for designers and illustrators, adopted certification, including a code very much based upon on our Canadian solution. And so, in May 2008, I took great pride in speaking at the first meeting of certified graphic designers in Oslo – where their new code of ethics was released – to essentially tell them this story I have been telling you, exactly **twenty years** after the week it began.

As I hurriedly finish up this book's text in the darkened audience of a design conference, listening to a new generation of remarkable creatives speak of how they will change the world, an e-mail arrives from Richard Grefé: AIGA's China office has established our revised *Standards of Professional Practice* as a template for over half a million design students in China.

So, don't tell me one person can't make a difference.

One person: the girlfriend who cared about how design affects her world.

One person: the guy who agreed design is political, and wrote a manifesto.

One person: the woman who spoke up at the meeting once she heard she was not alone.

One person: what's stopping *you?*

"The best time to plant a tree is twenty years ago. The second best time is now." CHINESE PROVERB

NOTES

All $ in this book indicate U.S. dollars.

1   Something positive that came out of Germany in 1938: the DIN typeface, named for the Deutsches Institut für Normung. In the mid-1990s Albert Jan-Pool, at the urging of Erik Spiekermann, refined the DIN typeface, and we use a mixture of DIN and Jan-Pool's DIN Pro from 2007 for our headings and supporting type. The body type of the book is set in the Meta Serif family, with a sprinkling of Meta Sans, both designed by Erik Spiekermann in 2007.

2   The Chinese Edition is published by Posts & Telecommunications Press, Beijing.

CHAPTER 1: START NOW

3   Yes, Scott, the fonts got substituted: it was a shocker on my first day in China. Not to worry: we fixed it later.

4   It is in vogue to refer to graphic design as "communication design" since the word "graphic" literally limits it to printing, while graphic designers work in many media. However, the new term suggests satellites and mobile phones to many: we'll see what wins. I'll lean toward "graphic design" in this book, to avoid confusion.

5   The earliest hero of the branding resistance movement must be Samuel Augustus Maverick, who moved to Texas in the 1800s and became famous for not branding his cattle. Unbranded cattle became known as mavericks. The Maverick family has been active in progressive politics for generations, including U.S. congressman Fontaine Maury Maverick. "Who You Callin' a Maverick?" by John Schwartz, *New York Times*, October 5, 2008.

6   Yes, of course I realize that classifying her as "hot" is sexist. This endnote is for anyone who misses the irony and is thinking of calling me on it. It's also to convince you that the endnotes might prove fun to read if you're a keener.

7   President George W. Bush radio address, March 22, 2003.

8   For a deep study of U.S. election design reform, *read Design for Democracy: Ballot + Election Design,* by Marcia Lausen, 2007.

9   Pat Buchanan interviewed on NBC's *Today*, November 9, 2000.

10   David's interview with Jessica Friedman Hewitt, managing director, Design For Democracy, September 2008. To see more samples and learn more about this, visit www.designfordemocracy.org.

11   Interview for "The Persuaders," *Frontline*, PBS, 2005. www.pbs.org/wgbh/pages/frontline/shows/persuaders/interviews/

12   Federal Election Chairman Michael Toner estimate, "Death Knell May Be Near for Public Election Funds," by David Kirkpatrick, *The New York Times*, January 23, 2007.

13   President Obama's campaign spent more than $250 million in the last four months of the 2008 campaign, outspending all U.S. advertisers except AT&T and Verizon on an annualized basis. That's more than McDonald's, Target, or Wal-Mart. "Obama spending more on ads than all but AT&T and Verizon," CNN, October 24, 2008.

14   Absentee ballot, Cuyahoga County, Ohio, U.S. General Election 2004.

15   35th of countries included in a study of electoral turnout in national lower house elections 1965-1995, from Mark N. Franklin's "Electoral Participation," found in *Controversies in Voting Behavior* (2001).

16   *A Regulatory Proposal To Include Warnings In Tobacco Advertisements*, Health Canada, November 2004.

17    $13.4 billion, as per fact sheet at www.tobaccofreekids.org.

18   *A Short History Of Progress*, Ronald Wright, 2004.

19   *A Short History Of Progress*, Ronald Wright, 2004.

20   Excerpt from *Maclean's* magazine, 1942.

21   *Earth In Mind*, David Orr, 2004.

22   Statement from 1965, in reference to *Operating Manual for Spaceship Earth*, Buckminster Fuller, 1963.

CHAPTER 2: BEYOND GREEN: A CONVENIENT LIE

23   1.2 billion 8-oz. servings of Coca-Cola soft drinks are consumed daily around the world. "Coke's Sinful World," Paul Klebnikov, *Forbes*, December 12, 2003.

24   Philip Morris International shipped 322.1 billion cigarettes in 2005, according to www.answers.com.

25   McDonald's Canada Web site FAQ, 2006.

26   BBC's h2g2 article on the ballpoint pen, 14,000,000 million BIC Crystals alone are sold daily.

27   To bottle water each year, 2.7 million tons of plastic are used worldwide, according to New American Dream's Web site. Only 14 percent of these bottles used in the U.S. are recycled, according to the Container Recycling Institute.

28   According to Greenpeace, an area of ancient forest the size of a football pitch (soccer field) is destroyed every two seconds.

29   "...every day, the equivalent of a major earthquake killing over 30,000 young children occurs to a disturbingly muted response. They die quietly in some of the poorest villages on earth, far removed from the scrutiny and the conscience of the world. Being meek and weak in life makes these dying multitudes even more invisible in death." *Progress of Nations*, UNICEF, 2000.

30   During 2007, 2.7 million people became infected with HIV, which causes AIDS (UNAIDS 2008 Report on the global AIDS epidemic).

31   Each year, approximately 300 to 500 million malaria infections lead to over one million deaths, of which 75 percent occur in African children. *Bulletin of the World Health Organization*, 1999, 77(8):624-40.

32   *Harvard Business Review* on Brand Management, 1999.

33   A report from the World Health Organization estimates that more than 600 lives are lost and more than 45,000 people are injured on China's roads every day.

34   According to UNICEF South Africa's current Web site, 300,000 babies are born to HIV positive mothers in South Africa annually. A 2006 study in the KwaZulu-Natal province (reported by John Donnelly in the *Boston Globe* on August 27, 2007) found a 20.6 percent HIV transmission rate from mother to child is 61,800 babies a year and 169 a day... which I round down to 160, for the sake of potential error in extrapolation.

35   Based on Edward O. Wilson's estimates of 27,000 species lost a year. (*The Diversity of Life*, 1992.) Niles Eldridge estimates 30,000 a year (*Life in the Balance: Humanity and the Biodiversity Crisis*, 1998).

36   Measured in constant dollars. *How Much Is Enough?*, Alan Durning, 1992.

37   *The Guardian*, September 2, 2005.

38 "Uncle Sam Wants You... to Go Shopping": A Consumer Society Responds to National Crisis, 1957-2001, by Robert H. Zieger, *Canadian Review of American Studies* 34.1, 2004.

39 Americans are storing more stuff than ever, by Tom Vanderbilt, *Slate*, July 18, 2005.

40 About two-thirds of American adults are overweight, and almost one-third are obese, according to data from the National Health and Nutrition Examination Survey (NHANES) 2001 to 2004.

41 CBC Radio, 2004.

42 Fallon Minneapolis won Plan Of The Year award for this work. *Brandweek*, June 18, 2001.

43 That many seconds of first quarter year prime time audience was selling for $840,000 (2005 *Thumbnail Media Planner*).

44 RealtyTrac Inc. of Irvine, CA (as reported by Associated Press).

45 Tim O'Reilly, O'Reilly Media, speech at Web 2.0 Expo, New York City, September 18, 2008.

46 *An Inconvenient Truth*, Al Gore, 2006.

47 "Measuring Brand Meaning," by Peter Dacin, Edward Blair, Betsy Gelb and Gillian Oakenfull, *Journal of Advertising Research*, September/October 2000.

48 Liberation can be about striking off shackles from someone's ankle, it can be about freeing someone from isolation or ignorance, it can be about providing choices. Visit www.davidberman.com/courses/accessibility for a comprehensive list of online resources regarding accessible technology.

CHAPTER 3: POP LANDSCAPE

49 The Coca-Cola Company Annual Report, 1995.

50 1.2 billion 8-oz. servings of Coca-Cola soft drinks are consumed daily around the world. "Coke's Sinful World," by Paul Klebnikov, *Forbes*, December 12, 2003.

51 "The Cola Conquest," DLI Productions for CBC, 1998.

52 You too can experience the entire Tanzanian adventure of Paul, David, and Spice the Cat! Visit www.paulgross.com/tanzania today!

53 "Coca-Cola has bigger plans for Tanzania," by Mgeta Mganga, *The Guardian* (Tanzania), July 16, 2005.

54 Tanzania ranks 156 of 179 ranked countries GDP per capita (PPP), *CIA World Factbook*, 2008.

55 *CIA World Factbook*, July 2008 estimate.

56 World Health Organization statistics, compiled at www.theglobalfund.org.

57 "Pop: Truth and Power at the Coca-Cola Company," *African Business*, April 1, 2004. John Pemberton, Coca-Cola's inventor, claimed the drink cured many diseases, including morphine addiction, dyspepsia, neurasthenia, headache, and impotence. Ironically Pemberton sold the rights to his famous recipe while himself suffering from a morphine addiction.

58 59.7 percent of Tanzania's population lives on under $2 a day, according to the World Bank, 1993.

59 *The Africa Malaria Report,* World Health Organization – UNICEF joint report.

60 *The Coca-Cola Company Annual Report*, 2003.

61 "Chain Reaction: From Einstein to the Atomic Bomb," in *Discover*, March, 2008.

62 Texas Rangers fans got their stadium back from now-bankrupt Ameriquest in 2007.

63 "Visual Pollution," in *The Economist*, October 11, 2007.

64 "A City Without Ads," in *Adbusters* #73.

CHAPTER 4: THE WEAPONS: VISUAL LIES AND MANUFACTURED NEEDS

65 And this is a graphic designer telling you this!

66 DBD Needham.

67 ...manufactured with European slave labor.

68 Marty Neumeier refers to this compromise as "wandering brand focus." For more examples, I urge you to read his classic The Brand Gap, another great AIGA Press / New Riders title.

69 If you're not already reading *Adbusters*, try it out.

70 I would have learned more birds had I been an NFL football fan.
    Pop quiz: how many? (answer at bottom of page)

71 *Harvard Business Review*, 1999.

72 Reproduced with permission from *@issue: The Journal of Business & Design*, published by Corporate Design Foundation and sponsored by Sappi. Visit www.cdf.org for more information about *@issue*.

73 Denver *Rocky Mountain News*, January 24, 2000.

74 *United Nations Human Development Report*, 1998.

75 *American Business Review*, June 1999... that's more than the annual GNP of the country of Jordan.

76 *Rules For Basketball*, 1892.

77 According to *Brands and Branding* (by Rita Clifton, John Simmons, and Sameena Ahmad, 2004), the seminal event for branding appearing on the balance sheet was when England's Reckitt & Colman purchased Airwick in 1985. Such activity prompted the London Stock Exchange to endorse brand valuation in 1989.

78 "'02-03 NBA Merchandise Sales From Outside U.S. Over $600M," *Sports Business Daily*

CHAPTER 5: WHERE THE TRUTH LIES: THE SLIPPERY SLOPE

79 *Intelligent Image Processing*, Steve Mann, 2002.

80 It is notable that the Morton Salt girl has been getting thinner and leggier over the years, becoming more akin to the more sexualized Coppertone girl (in her permanent state of innocently losing her bathing suit to her dog).

81 *BusinessWeek*, August, 2005

82 Yes, it's generally spelled "whiskey" for Irish and American products, "whisky" for Scottish, Canadian, and Japanese.

83 *Is This Life – Or Is It Just Memorex*, by Bruce Brown, inaugural GLAD lecture (National Association of Graphic Design Educators), 1997.

84 *The Washington Post*, July 15, 1991. According to the *The Times* of London, the four Amway distributors who launched the rumor were ordered to pay $20 million in damages in March, 2007.

85 R.J.Rummell estimates that in all centuries preceding the 20th century, democides accounted for 133 million deaths, compared to 192 million for the 20th century. "Statistics of Democide: Genocide and Mass Murder Since 1900," R.J. Rummell, 1997.

86 David Berman interview with head of Copperhead Brewing Company, Ottawa, 1994.

87   500,000 breast implant procedures are performed a year in Colombia.

88   Avon and other companies profit from direct sales in Brazil and other developing countries. "Perfuming the Amazon," *The Economist* (U.S. edition), October 22, 1994.

89   Fact is (and I'll leave the images to your imagination), Muhammad appeared in German advertising for bouillon extract in 1928, as well as in a promotion of Ogden's cigarettes. Or ask the bas-relief sculptor who carved the image of Mohammed into the North Frieze of the Supreme Court building standing right now in Washington, D.C.

90   *Canada Health Action: Building on the Legacy*, Health Canada, 2004.

CHAPTER 6: WINE, WOMEN, AND WATER   No notes

CHAPTER 7: LOSING OUR SENSES

91   In Kenya, the land of President Obama's father, the Senator beer brand, known locally as "Obama" was launched the same month that Obama won his senate seat, providing a local and relatively affordable alternative, served only from kegs, to the often-lethal cornmeal-based chang'aa. The Kenyan government rescinded excise taxes to help keep the beer affordable in the interests of public health. In "Kenya, Obama (Beer) Wins Big," by Eliza Barclay, *BusinessWeek*, March 26, 2008.

92   *No Logo,* Naomi Klein, 2000.

93   Brand logo recognition by children aged 3 to 6 years. "Mickey Mouse and Old Joe the Camel," by P. M. Fischer, M. P. Schwartz, J. W. Richards Jr, A.O. Goldstein and T. H. Rojas, *JAMA*, December 1991.

94   The font family is called Marlboro, allegedly custom-designed for the campaign, though it sure looks like Neo Contact (FontShop font 127957 from URW).

95   *Altria 2004 Annual Report.*

96   *No Logo,* Naomi Klein, 2000.

97   It just is.

98   "Why Tony still has a grip on kids' diets," by Andrew Duffy, *The Ottawa Citizen*, February 11, 2008.

99   "Potential effects of the next 100 billion hamburgers sold by McDonald's," by E. H. Spencer, *American Journal of Preventative Medicine*, May, 2005.

100 More so if by volume. *How Much Is Enough,* Alan Durning, 1992.

101 *The Washington Monthly.*

102 Dr. Kelly Brownell, Yale University.

103 $230 a year. *State of the World 1991,* Worldwatch Institute, Washington, D.C.

104 Agenda Inc., Paris/San Francisco. www.agendainc.com.

105 "Children, adolescents and advertising" policy statement, American Academy of Pediatrics, 1995; Kunkel, 2001; Macklin & Carlson [eds], 1999, as cited in Strasburger, *Developmental and Behavioral Pediatrics*, 2001.

106 Final report of the health committee of Canada's House of Commons, March, 2006.

107 *No Logo,* Naomi Klein, 2000.

CHAPTER 8: WHY OUR TIME IS THE PERFECT TIME

108 *@issue Journal*, Volume 1, Number 1, Corporate Design Foundation.

109 *Nova*, Public Broadcasting Service, 2000.

110 "Honda Civic Now America's Best-Selling Vehicle," in *USNews & World Report*, June 4, 2008.

111 Happily, this number is dropping as hybrids and other alternative vehicles designs become ubiquitous.

112 The Exxon Valdez settlement was drastically reduced; the Florida suit was dismissed in class action form, but individual cases were upheld and the finding that tobacco companies had concealed information and acted negligently was supported.

113 Physicians for a Smoke-Free Canada director Cynthia Callard credits a series of anti-smoking policies since the late 1990s for the continuing drop. The policies include larger and more foreboding warnings on cigarettes. "Smoking Falls to All-Time Low In Canada," in *Ottawa Citizen*, August 12, 2005.

114 "How to circumvent tobacco advertising restrictions: the irrelevance of the distinction between direct and indirect advertising," by Luk Joossens, March 2001.

115 There were 4,000 of these types of fires in 2000, resulting in CDN$56.7 million in losses, according to the Canada Safety Council.

116 U.S. National Fire Protection Association's Web site, accessed July 2008.

117 If you haven't read Edward Tufte, I urge you to do so. This statistician-turned-information designer is a champion of the ethics of preparing information in clear and truthful ways. Start with his classic *The Visual Display of Quantitative Information*, 1982.

118 "The Hundred-Dollar Laptop," by Jason Pontin, *Technology Review*, August 2005.

CHAPTER 9: HOW TO LIE, HOW TO TELL THE TRUTH

119 Study by Media Awareness Network, Ottawa, 2005.

CHAPTER 10: HOW WE DO GOOD IS HOW WE DO GOOD

120 According to the BBC's h2g2, 14,000,000 million BIC Crystals alone are sold daily.

121 www.oddcopy.net.

122 Management report of BIC Board of Directors for 2003 (U.S.).

123 *Cradle To Cradle*, William McDonough & Michael Braungart, 2002.

CHAPTER 11: PROFESSIONAL CLIMATE CHANGE

124 Icograda is the International Council of Graphic Design Associations, IFI is the International Federation of Interior Architects/Designers, and icsid is the International Council of Societies of Industrial Design.

125 "The New Annual Report," in *@issue* Volume 13, Number 1, Spring 2008.

CHAPTER 12: "WHAT CAN ONE PROFESSIONAL DO?"

126 Personal interview with managing director, Icograda, 2007.

127 Your endnote here... you too can be an author: the author of your own life. What can you do today with your professional skill and opportunity to help create the legacy you wish to leave?

INDEX

"You don't finish writing a book; you abandon it." – Carolyn Brown

QUESTIONS FOR DISCUSSION

1. What initiatives require a group of designers, rather than just one, to be successful?

2. When is sexy okay in an advertisement? Or a magazine cover?

3. Should designers be certified?

4. When is it okay for a designer to say no?

5. If you could pass one law to help address the largest challenge presented, what would it be?

6. What parts of the Do Good Pledge could best be embraced by all professions?

7. Mecca-Cola is now available in the Middle East. Is it okay to appropriate Mecca to get out from under Coke's cultural monopoly?

8. How can social networking technologies be used to help craft ethical solutions?

9. Is helping to design an ad for an SUV fundamentally unethical?

10. Once the environmental crisis is solved, what is the next greatest threat that designers should help solve?

11. What *is* stopping you?

ACKNOWLEDGMENTS
A SMALL GROUP OF COMMITTED CITIZENS

"The success of any kind of social epidemic is heavily dependent on the involvement of people with a particular and rare set of social skills."

MALCOLM GLADWELL

Thank you to all these souls and organizations that have helped facilitate this work, and none more so than Cynthia Hoffos who has tirelessly and lovingly brought it from grey to black and white.

Arturo de Albornoz (Mexico City)
Birgitte Appelong (Oslo)
Ben Armitage (Ottawa)
Hilary Ashworth (Toronto)
Walid Azzi (Beirut)
Anna Barton (Praha)
Dr. Eli Berman (San Diego)
Hannah Langford Berman (Ottawa)
Reva Berman (Ottawa)
Dr. Shier Berman (Ottawa)
Shirley Berman (Ottawa)
Diego Bermudez (Bogotá)
Sherry Blankenship (Doha)
Karen Blincoe (Devon)
Carlo Branzaglia (Bologna)
Eren Butler (London)
Peggy Cady, FGDC (Victoria)
Leonardo Castillo (Recife)
Don Ryun Chang (Seoul)
Brian M. Chee (Daegu)
Halim Choueiry (Jounieh)
Amy Chow (Hong Kong)
David Coates, FGDC (Vancouver)
Christopher Comeau (Ottawa)
Matt Cowley (Toronto)
Patrick Cunningham (Ottawa)
Sara Curtis (Toronto)
Du Qin (Beijing)

Éric Dupuis (Montréal)
Steve Eichler (Calgary)
Ray Farmilo (Ottawa)
Chantal Fontaine (Montréal)
Dr. Alan Frank (Ottawa)
Gao Gao (Beijing)
Catherine Garden, FGDC (Calgary)
Andrea Gardner (Ottawa)
Ken Garland (London)
Amy Gendler (Beijing)
Shaun George (New Minas)
Piedad Gomez (Bogotá)
Richard Grefé (New York)
Paul Gross (Ottawa)
David Grossman (Tel Aviv)
Kenroy Harrison (Tokyo)
Zelda Harrison (Los Angeles)
Jessica Friedman Hewitt (New York)
Anne Mette Hoel (Oslo)
Cynthia Hoffos, FGDC (Ottawa)
Jannicke Hølen (Oslo)
Ryan Iler (Ottawa)
Lene Vad Jensen (København)
Trevor Johnston (Ottawa)
Russell Kennedy (Melbourne)
Pete Kercher (Como)
Jinwon Kim (Seoul)
Warren Kinsella (Calgary)

Kris Klaasen (Vancouver)
Lise Vejse Klint (København)
Ruth Klotzel (São Paolo)
Mervyn Kurlansky (Hornbæk)
Jacques Lange (Tshwane)
Lee Nawon (Seoul)
Marc Lefkowitz (København)
László Lelkes (Budapest)
Liu Bo (Beijing)
Felipe Cesar Londoño (Manizales)
Boris Ljubičić (Zagreb)
Sabina Lysnes (Thunder Bay)
Mary Ann Maruska, FGDC (Oakville)
Peter Martin and his camel (Doha)
Rod Nash, R.G.D. (Toronto)
Jan Neste (Oslo)
Paul Nishikawa, MGDC (Calgary)
Ian Noble (London)
Robert L. Peters, FGDC (Winnipeg)
Tomasz Pirc (Maribor)
Steven Rosenberg, FGDC (Winnipeg)
Thomas Rymer (Moscow)
Hashem Salameh (Bahrain)
Brenda Sanderson, MGDC (Montréal)
Mike Shahin (Ottawa)
Sudhir Sharma (Mumbai)
Leslie Shelman (Cambridge)
Scott Sigurdson (Ottawa)
Steve Spalding (Gainesville)
Erik Spiekermann (Berlin)
Jan Stavik (Oslo)
Marie Stradeski (Cape Breton)
Anne Telford (San Francisco)
Sophie Thomas (London)
Peggy Varner (Ottawa)
Omar Vulpinari (Milano)
Joel Wachman (Cambridge)
Min Wang (China)
Matt Warburton, FGDC (Vancouver)
William Warren (London)
Kernaghan Webb (Toronto)
Matt Wills (Richford)
Matt Woolman (Richmond)
Xiao Yong (Beijing)
Zheng Tao (Beijing)

Adbusters Media Foundation
(Canada)
AIGA (United States)
Applied Arts (Canada)
Association of Registered Graphic
Designers of Ontario (Canada)
C3 Design (Canada)
California Department of Public
Health (United States)
Central Academy of Fine Arts (China)
Concordia University (Canada)
EIDD (Europe)
Federal University of Pernambuco
(Brazil)
The Globe & Mail (Canada)
Grafill (Norway)
Hong Kong Design Centre
(Hong Kong)
Hungarian Academy of Fine Arts
(Hungary)
ICIS (Denmark)
Icograda (Earth)
Ikea (Norway)
Kontrapunkt (Denmark)
Lebanese American University
(Lebanon)
Leo Burnett (South Africa)
London College of Communication
(United Kingdom)
Magdalena Festival (Slovenia)
Norwegian Design Council (Norway)
Origin Instruments (United States)
Sanford Corporation (United States)
Sappi Papers (South Africa)
Society of Graphic Designers of
Canada (Canada)
Union for Democratic
Communications (United States)
Universidad de Caldas (Colombia)
Virginia Commonwealth University
(United States, Qatar)
Wallpaper (United Kingdom)
Yarmouk University (Jordan)
Your local bottler of Coca-Cola
(within reach of wherever you are)

ABOUT THE AUTHOR

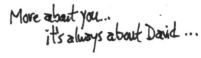

More about you..
it's always about David...

DAVID BERMAN has 30 years of experience as designer and strategist. He provides motivation and techniques for applying strategy, design thinking, ethics, and creative branding and communications to business problems.

His award-winning client list includes IBM, the International Space Station, Health Canada, the Aga Khan Foundation, the Sierra Club, the Canadian Broadcasting Corporation, Canadian Air Transport Security Authority, and Canada's three largest Web sites.

He has had a longtime passion for accessible, universal design, with projects for governments, private sector, and schools on five continents.

In 2009, he was appointed a high-level advisor to the United Nations on how design can help fulfill the Millennium Development Goals. He joined the ISO committee for universally-accessible PDF format in 2011. In 2012, he became a Chair for accessible technology at Carleton University.

Since 1984, he has worked to establish codes of ethical practice that embrace social responsibility for designers throughout Canada and the world. He served as the first elected president of the Association of Registered Graphic Designers of Ontario from 1997 to 1999. David drafted the association's constitution and Rules of Professional Conduct, as well as the section of the certification exam on professional responsibility.

In 1999, he was named a Fellow of the Society of Graphic Designers of Canada, the country's top honor in the profession, and was elected national ethics chair in 2000, a role he continues in today.

David served three terms on the board of Icograda, the world body for communication design, and is now their Sustainability Chair. He is also a professional member of AIGA, IFPS, a Friend of IEDD, and Lifelong Member of Grafill.

Perhaps his greatest professional passion is as expert speaker: he keynotes on the role professionals can play in improving the human condition and the global environment. David's speaking and professional journey has brought him to over 50 countries.

Visit www.davidberman.com/about for more about David, or to involve him in the success of your project or event. Or e-mail david@davidberman.com.

 linkedin.com/in/bermandavid

ONLINE ACCESS TO THIS BOOK

With the purchase of this book you get instant online, searchable limited access to its **electronic edition** at Safari Books Online.

1. Visit www.peachpit.com/safarienabled
2. Enter code NKHVKEH to get your free online access